EGYPTIAN MYSTERIES

Order From
THE SURVIVAL CENTER
P.O. Box 234
McKenna, WA 98558

EGYPTIAN MYSTERIES

An Account of an Initiation

SAMUEL WEISER, INC.
York Beach, Maine

First published in English in 1988 by
Samuel Weiser, Inc.
Box 612
York Beach, Maine 03910

Second printing, 1991

English translation © 1988 Samuel Weiser, Inc.
All rights reserved. No part of this work may be reproduced or
transmitted in any form or by any means, electronic or mechanical,
including photocopy, without permission in writing from Samuel
Weiser, Inc. Reviewers may quote brief passages.

First published in Dutch in 1981 by
Uitgeverij Schors, Amsterdam, Holland,
under the title: *Egyptische Mysterien:
Verslag van een Inwijding*
© 1981 W.N. Schors

Library of Congress Cataloging-in-Publication Data:

Egyptian mysteries.

    Often attributed to Iamblichus.
    1. Initiation rites—Egypt. 2. Mysteries, Religious.
I. Iamblichus, ca. 250-ca. 330.
BL2443.E34   1988   291.3'8   88-104
                                              CIP

ISBN 0-87728-681-7
CCP

Printed in the United States of America

Contents

Foreword vii
Introduction xiii

Part One: THE INITIATION

The Tests 3

Part Two: THE SECRETS

The First Symbol 39
The Second Symbol 45
The Third Symbol 49
The Fourth Symbol 55
The Fifth Symbol 59
The Sixth Symbol 63
The Seventh Symbol 65
The Eighth Symbol 69

The Ninth Symbol 73
The Tenth Symbol 77
The Eleventh Symbol 87
The Twelfth Symbol 93
The Thirteenth Symbol 97
The Fourteenth Symbol 103
The Fifteenth Symbol 109
The Sixteenth Symbol 113
The Seventeenth Symbol 119
The Eighteenth Symbol 125
The Nineteenth Symbol 129
The Twentieth Symbol 135
The Twenty-First Symbol 141
The Twenty-Second Symbol 151

Foreword

Egyptian Mysteries is an intriguing text, for little is known about the author, when or how it was written, or even about the purpose of the book.

In the occult world it is generally accepted that it was written by Iamblichus, the Neo-Platonist and most important representative of the Alexandrian School. This view seems unfounded. In the first place, the title of the book by Iamblichus (fourth century A.D.) is *On the Mysteries, particularly those of the Egyptians, Chaldeans and the Assyrians*, and in the second place, that fourth century work deals with eternal mystical and philosophical questions of the creation of the cosmos, and the relationship between the creator and the created — it does not contain any fragments or references to an initiation ritual.

However, it is not surprising that *Egyptian Mysteries* has been linked with Iamblichus. Like Apollonius of Tyana, he, too, was known as a great magician with many paranormal gifts. For example, there is the story of how he created the principles of Eros and Anteros from the hot springs at Gadara in the shape of two young men. He was also able to depict events very clearly and could contact the Creator by means of theurgic ceremonies. Thus, he was familiar with the meaning and content of initiation rituals, particularly as during the early days of Christianity these still played an important role in the many schools of mystery. However, despite all this, his work bears no resemblance to the text given in this book: the translations of Iamblichus by Taylor (1821), Quillard (1895), and Hopfner (1921) do not contain a single passage which is related to or identical with this material.

When the American occultist and founder of the Brotherhood of Light, Elbert Benjamine, wrote in 1901 that his friend Genevieve Stebbins had translated the French edition of Iamblichus's *Egyptian Mysteries* for her friends, he was in error, though the mistake was made in good faith and is very understandable.

The French edition was supposedly translated *from the original manuscript* by the French occultist, Christian, the pseudonym of Jean-Baptiste Pitois, the author of the famous *L'Homme Rouge des Tuileries*.

There is absolutely no doubt that Christian translated an esoteric text of great value. As a librarian responsible for sorting out countless books and manuscripts which had fallen into the possession of the French state after the confiscation of monastic libraries, and as an esoteric scholar—his knowledge of astrology came from his friend Honoré de Balzac, and his insight into the Cabala, magic and tarot from his mentor, Eliphas Levi—he was the ideal person to assess the spiritual value of manuscripts.

In other words, *Egyptian Mysteries* was very probably translated into French by Christian, though not *from the original manuscript* (how many fourth century manuscripts have survived?) but from a handwritten copy, many of which had been circulating in the occult world from the Middle Ages up to the 19th century.

It is characteristic of the particular value which Christian himself assigned the manuscript that he never officially published his translation. The works cited by Paul Chacornac, biographer of Eliphas Levi, and erudite occultist par excellence, do not mention an initiation ritual by an author such as Iamblichus. We therefore conclude that like Genevieve Stebbins, Christian circulated a limited edition of a manuscript ascribed to Iamblichus which dealt with an initiation ritual, because he considered that an official publication would reveal too much about the content of such initiations. Those who later used his translation, whether they belonged to the American Brotherhood of Light or other French or German esoteric schools, also endeavored to be careful not to publish more than romanticized fragments, excerpts, or isolated conclusions.

The question that will undoubtedly arise is how Christian, and many others with him, could believe that the text was truly by Iamblichus. Curiously, the answer is to be found in the history of Iamblichus's *Mysteries* itself. Just as the Egyptian character is deliberately emphasized there because everything that was believed to have come from Egypt was automatically viewed with respect and not thrown into the trash can by the Church Fathers as heresy, the name of Iamblichus was probably added to *Egyptian Mysteries* in the belief that the text would gain authenticity, and therefore influence, as a result. Moreover, figures like Christian and Eliphas Levi, followers of Count de Gebelin and Fabre D'Olivet, were always inclined to seek the origins of any esoteric material either in Egypt or Israel.

The late 18th century German manuscript, on which this edition is based, is very similar to two types of manuscripts that were circulating amongst occultists at that time. One type was based on the doctrines and rituals of Cagliostro's *Egyptian Freemasonry*, the other on the initiation rituals of the Illuminati, a partly political, partly occult German society. The real intentions of Cagliostro or of Weishaupt and Von Knigge (the founders of the Order of Illuminati) are not particularly relevant in this context. However, it is relevant that both societies developed to a peak of activity in the 1780's, and that both were far from reluctant to use mysterious, terrifying initiation rituals based on the idea that true followers could only be found if they were able to withstand the demanding tests. The element of cruelty, which is often reminiscent of the tortures of the puberty rites of Indians and Africans, is not present in most other initiation rituals, which tend to emphasize the initiation.

On the other hand, the element of threat is so much in the foreground in *Egyptian Mysteries* that we are inclined to believe that we are not concerned here with a ritual handed down from antiquity, or by the

Rosicrucians or Freemasons, but with a type of initiation introduced either by Cagliostro or even earlier by the Illuminati, permeated with elements of Neo-Platonism and theosophy. This means that it not only remains plausible, but also gives the impression of being centuries old and of Egyptian origin, an impression reinforced by the terminology.

To summarize: this text was probably drawn up at the end of the 18th century in the circles of the Illuminati with the intention of creating a hard core of initiates prepared to disseminate the Order's ideas at any price. Whatever doubts one might have about this, it cannot be said that the initiation describes conflicts with any of the traditions, and it takes into account the occult laws, also from a chronological point of view.

As detailed descriptions of initiations are extremely rare — one of the few valuable exceptions is *The Most Sacred Threefold Wisdom*, of which one copy was impounded after the Inquisition imprisoned Cagliostro in Rome — we feel that it is worthwhile to produce an English translation of this initiation. In addition, the text provides an opportunity to consider whether the act of initiation, itself, still has a place in our time.

If initiation is seen as a method for altering states of consciousness, obviously it can still be meaningful today, because many people are aware that another and greater existence lies behind their prosaic everyday lives. If you have ever been in love, you know that the monotonous grind of reality can change at a stroke into a world of glowing joy, simply because you've met someone special. This is no sensory illusion. It is a real state that we could live all the time if we did not let ourselves be overwhelmed by drudgery, frustration, desire, or loss of morale. Religious people are also familiar with moments of recognition of another world characterized by a blissful feeling of balance and peace.

Initiation is aimed at a lasting renewal. This is the difference between esoteric study on the one hand, and modern therapeutic methods on the other. For where modern psychology endeavors to help people feel more comfortable with themselves, esoteric studies show that behind human endeavor lies a world of unlimited psychic possibilities and content. Self-knowledge is the first step in the discovery and control of that world — a constant renewal can only be acquired by means of step-by-step development, which is characteristic of initiation.

Introduction

The creation of the religious beliefs to which Egypt owes its great fame is shrouded in mystery, as is the creation of the nation itself. Only the monuments which have survived through the ages irrefutably prove that theocracy was the system of government that held sway in Egypt. It is also certain that since time immemorial the Egyptian priest was both a servant of God and a servant of science, in this way fulfilling the two most important tasks entrusted to humanity—the work of the spirit and the work of reason. Supreme power was in the hands of a High Priest or Hierophant (Keeper of the Sacred Word), whose commands in the name of God were transmitted and obeyed by the priests devoted to Him.

Originally Thebes, the holy city in Upper Egypt, was the center of the nation, but as a result of the steady increase in population, outposts were gradually established ever further southwards along the Nile, until in due course the Nile Delta was also inhabited by Egyptians.

The nation was divided into four classes or social strata, consisting of priests, soldiers, merchants and workers. The soldiers, who were, of course, not a productive class, were supported by the other classes to defend national security, and spent most of their time arrogantly doing nothing. From behind the might and power of their weapons they suppressed the spiritual leaders and under Menes finally even proclaimed a monarchy, exchanging the tiara of the priest for the crown of a king. In this way Menes became the founder of the Egyptian dynasties, and in this capacity he can be found at the head of the list of reigning monarchs who were documented on ancient papyri and monuments by the priest Manathon.

The priests were deprived of their ruling power, but it soon became apparent that for a nation educated in a religious tradition, the power of the monarchy alone was insufficient and was not absolute enough to have any spiritual effect. Meanwhile knowledge and understanding, the domain of the priests, developed in its own way, for the knowledge could not be suppressed or forced in any way by a revolution. Thebes, the great center, did not lose any of its influence or prestige, and Menes eventually considered it necessary to found his own capital city, which had to be very heavily defended, for his authority was based only on military strength. This new city was named Memphis, and for some time it was one of the most important centers in Egypt. Curiously, nothing remains of this city in the ruins between Cairo and

Sakkara. Even the location of Memphis remains a mystery; the silt of the Nile and the sand of the desert have covered it completely, while the impressive ruins of Thebes survive to fascinate the traveler and provide an inkling of the majestic glory of ancient days.

The Pyramids

Three monuments survive on the plateau of Giza, opposite Cairo on the left bank of the Nile, which have withstood the ravages of time wonderfully well. These are the pyramids, three massive structures built on a square base, each slightly different in size and forming a triangle in the way they are sited, with one side facing north, one side facing west and the third side facing east.

The largest pyramid is in the north opposite the delta and is a symbol of the force of nature. The second is in the southeast, an arrow's flight away from the first, a symbol of movement, while the last, in the southwest is a stone's throw from the second and is a symbol of time.

Three smaller pyramids are situated in the vicinity of this last great pyramid and an enormous pile of rubble nearby suggests that there must have been a seventh pyramid which did not survive the ravages of time. It is likely that the ancient Egyptians used these seven monuments to represent the seven planetary spirits who were revealed to them by Thoth.

There is no proof regarding the origin of the pyramids. Herodotus, the father of Greek history, claimed that the Great Pyramid was built by Cheops. On the other hand, Deodorus states that it was built by Chemmis; George le Cyncella gives the builder as Souphis, while others still name Athotes, Thoth or Hermes as the possible architect. There is just as much uncertainty with regard to the other pyramids. The Jewish historian Flavius Josephus maintains—though without bothering to support his claim with a single shred of evidence—that the pyramids were built by the Jews before the exodus from Egypt, although other authors wrote that 365,000 workers toiled for forty-eight years on these monuments. The actual historical origins of the pyramids remain as a mystery that may never be answered, like so many of the riddles which consume the interests of archeologists.

The rock forming the base of the pyramids is situated about a hundred feet above the highest tidal point of the Nile. It is a mass of granite and its bottom has still not been found—even after all the excavations—some of which have gone as deep as 200 feet. The foundation of the Great Pyramid is about 750 feet long and it has a volume of about 75,000 cubic feet. Above the first course of stones, which is surrounded by a moat hewn into the rock in very regular manner, there are 202 further courses, each of which has been built slightly further in to form steps. The total number of steps gives the pyramid a height of 428 feet, but excavations have shown that in the course of time at least two steps have been worn down so that the pyramid was probably 450 feet high. The orientation of the pyramid bears witness to great accuracy: each of the corners faces one of the points of the compass. By means of this no less than perfect position it has been possible to establish that after several thousands of years there has been no noticeable change in the angle of the earth's axis, a fact which is of considerable importance for an understanding of the planet Earth.

In addition, it should be noted that the pyramid is the only monument on earth which makes it possible to verify such a fact.

The present entrance lies on the northeastern face at the level of the fifteenth course of stones, approximately 45 feet above the base. It was once possible to close this entrance with a flat stone which could slide from left to right by means of a special mechanism. This door opened onto a sloping corridor which ended in a high hall. There is a well in the middle of this hall which leads to two burial chambers.

In addition, the corridor provides access to corridors at a lower level, so that fresh air circulates through these by means of an ingenious system of ventilation. The burial chambers themselves contain two sarcophagi, neither of which has any inscriptions. As nearly all obelisks, ruined temples and tombs are amply covered with inscriptions, this suggests that the pyramids were built and the sarcophagi placed inside them before inscriptions became customary. Although modern research methods have made a great deal of progress, it remains a mystery how the Egyptian architects of the First Dynasty were able to build chambers and corridors in a massive structure which remain intact sixty centuries later, despite the millions of kilos weighing down upon them.

The Sphinx

When modern researchers attempted to uncover the foundation of this statue it became clear that the Sphinx had been hewn from the granite of the plateau a short distance from the Great Pyramid, rising from the granite and forming part of it.

In view of the enormous size — it is 75 feet high — it is not difficult to imagine the tremendous work that must have gone into clearing and leveling the space around it. The Sphinx is 120 feet long; the distance from the lower belly to the mouth is 50 feet, and from the mouth to the crown, 25 feet; the circumference of the head (around the forehead) measures 80 feet.

The difference in color of the various layers of granite from which the Sphinx has been hewn produces a very special effect in a unique way, particularly in the features. For example, the mouth of the Sphinx has been carved at a point where two layers of stone merge together. In addition, a hollow a feet few deep was made in the head, which probably served in ancient days for making sacrifices of incense or for holding a holy symbol, possibly a priest's tiara or a royal crown.

The Sphinx is slightly red in color, and, half buried under the sand, it still commands great respect. It has the appearance of a merciless, untouchable sentinel keeping guard over the pyramids. The legend of the Sphinx corroborates this impression. It is said to watch and listen; its great ears seem to be attuned to the rumbling of the past; the eyes peer deeply and fixedly toward the East, seeming to look into the future, and fascinating every visitor. A closer inspection reveals that this work — half statue, half hill — exudes exceptional majesty, great calm and even a degree of compassion.

Greek mythology, inspired by tales of the Sphinx brought back by travelers who had seen it in the distance, tells of a monstrous sphinx, half human and half wild beast, which, according to the fanciful tale, would present all travelers passing by with an insoluble riddle, and then devour those who were unable to answer. Despite this danger, Oedipus dared to undertake his perilous adventure to meet the Sphinx who asked him: "Which creature walks on four legs at sunrise, on two legs in the afternoon and on three in the evening?" The hero unhesitatingly answered: "Man." Certainly when day breaks—in other words, during the first few months of life, we move on hands and feet; at noon, when we are adults, we walk on two legs; and at dusk, when we are old and bowed down by the weight of our years, we use a cane to move around. The Sphinx, which no doubt had never come across such presence of mind, stared at Oedipus with mouth agape, giving the latter the opportunity to attack and kill the creature.

The childhood fable detracts from the enormous value of this fantastic symbol. Greek philosophers up to Plato did not understand its true content. Plato, a pupil of Socrates, was a brilliant philosopher widely known in his own time. He was initiated into the Mysteries of Hermes-Thoth by the magicians of Memphis.

Copies of the Sphinx can be found at the entrances to all the Egyptian temples, though the original, as mentioned earlier, stands in front of the pyramids. It is a stone enigma, a soundless introduction, a veiled key of knowledge, and we will attempt to trace its deeper meaning.

The etymological derivation of the word "sphinx" comprises the concept of "inclusion," and indeed this mighty statue can be viewed as a symbol of the four principles—earth, water, fire and air—which are frequently and quite incorrectly called "elements."

The statue, which is composed of the head of a woman, the body of a bull, the claws of a lion and the wings of an eagle, forms a fantastic whole, and once its symbolism starts to become clear, it no longer inspires fear but instills a sense of awe. The head can be interpreted as a symbol of human intelligence, which, before acting in a way that will determine the future, must examine the purpose of such action, must think of the ways of achieving this purpose, and the ways of avoiding obstacles and skirting round difficulties.

The bull, which forms the body, indicates that we are armed with knowledge, supported by an indefatigable will, and must tread the path leading to success step by step with strength of mind and patience through all trials. The claws of the lion show that in order to achieve the goal which has been set by reason, the will alone is not enough, and courage is at least as important. It is not sufficient merely to work, but often one must fight to attain a place in society.

The wings of the eagle teach us that we must keep our intentions to ourselves until we carry them out, when we must act as quickly and decisively as possible in a steadfast manner. The Hierophant said to the candidate:

> Learn to see clearly, learn to wish for what is just, learn to dare what your conscience dictates, learn to keep your intentions secret, and if, despite all your efforts, today brings no more than yesterday, do not lose courage, but continue steadfastly, keeping your goal before you with determination. Onward! The Seven Companions of the Soul—the planetary spirits—guard the sacred key

which locks the past and opens the future. Let your efforts be aimed at the Crown of the Master.

Seen in this light, the Sphinx cannot be viewed as an image of a deity, and certainly not as the bloodthirsty monster that inspired the Greek myths. It is a symbol of unpredictable strength, an example of human will led by crystal-clear intelligence. The Sphinx is alpha and omega, the first and last word of higher initiations.

Initiation into the Highest Knowledge was not open to just anyone — not even to any Egyptian priest. Before they were ready for the Highest Initiation, priests had to fulfill a number of tasks and pass a number of tests to be allowed to go through to the next level. Every test served as a measure of the level of intelligence and moral strength the candidate had acquired. Those who did not pass the test with flying colors the first time were denied once and for all the chance to try to fulfill the entrance requirements for higher levels. They were not permitted to take the examination a second time. Even the son of a magician could go no further than the point which he had been unable to pass, and would be given a position in one of the temples in accordance with his aptitude, without any remaining possibility of a more dignified position.

If a candidate was a stranger to the mysteries, an extremely strict inquiry would first be made into the candidate's ancestry, and if the result of this inquiry was favorable, the college of magicians would convene in a secret session to determine admission or rejection.

In the event of admission, the first test was actually so arduous that the candidate might be frightened off if he did not have a sufficiently strong will, and at this point he could still change his mind or withdraw. However, if he continued the initiation process and the first symbols of the secret knowledge were revealed to him and he was not able to pass one of the subsequent tests, he was condemned by an irrevocable and unchangeable law to die in the domain of the magicians. He would not be permitted to see daylight again.

The Greek philosophers—Thales, Pythagoras, Plato and Eudoxus—were the best-known foreign scholars to successfully pass the various tests. Pythagoras was assigned the prophet Sonchis as his mentor. According to the writings of Proclus, Plato was trained for thirteen years by Patheneith, Ochoaps, Sechthouphis, as well as other less well-known magicians. The brilliant teachings of Plato, who had an enormous influence on the development of Christian philosophy, originated in the sacred places of Memphis, the city of Menes, and in Heliopolis, the city of the sun.

Iamblichus, the well-known Greek philosopher who lived in Syria at the beginning of the fourth century, has left us a detailed description of the Egyptian mysteries, including the main tests to which aspiring initiates were subjected. Although the greatest secrets have obviously been omitted from these descriptions, what remains is nevertheless so valuable that the content must not remain unpublished.

In the following chapters we will travel with the aspiring initiate along the path of his trials step-by-step, and we will try to examine and understand the lessons that this path reveals for our own lives.

Part One

THE INITIATION

The Tests

According to ancient documents, the Sphinx, which stands near the Great Pyramid, served as an entrance to the vaults where the initiate was subjected to the tests of initiation before understanding the mysteries. The entrance, which is now buried under sand and rubble, can still be made out between the forepaws of this colossal guard. In the past, the entrance was closed with a bronze portal, which opened by means of a mechanism known only to the magicians. Because of its inaccessibility, the Sphinx commanded respect and inspired all onlookers with a sort of religious awe, which served as better protection than any armed guard.

The inside of the Sphinx contained various corridors which connected with the subterranean part of the Great Pyramid. These corridors had been built so ingeniously and criss-crossed so much that people who dared to penetrate this labyrinth unaccompanied would inevitably get lost and would be unable to find their way back without the help of the magicians. The construction of these corridors testifies to an exceptionally skilled architecture, which is still not surpassed today, even by complicated subway systems and railway networks.

The two oldest magicians, advanced both in age and rank, who fulfilled the role of Thesmothetes (or the Keeper of the Rites) were ordered to supervise the candidate who had been permitted by general consensus to take the tests. The initiate in turn had to submit to the discretion of his supervisors, listen to their advice and follow it as a command, and refrain from asking any questions. As soon as he passed through the doors of Memphis, the initiate was blindfolded so that he would not be able to reconstruct in his imagination either the path he trod or the distance or place where he was taken.

Let us assume that we are present at the initiation. The blindfolded candidate has now been led to the door between the forepaws of the Sphinx. The bronze door is opened and closes soundlessly behind them when one of the magicians operates the mechanism. The other supervisor takes a lamp from the wall to light the way. The initiate is taken by the hand toward a spiral staircase with twenty-two steps which he must descend. At the end of this staircase another bronze door opens and shuts, leading to a circular vault. This door, through which the initiate steps, is hidden in the wall of rock in such a way that we see nothing that might suggest an entrance. The initiation begins in this chamber.

The two supervisors suddenly and brusquely stop the initiate and make him believe that he is standing on the edge of an abyss and that if he takes one step forward he will plunge down.

One of the magicians insistently intones: "This abyss surrounds the Temple of Mysteries and guards it against the brazen curiosity of the profane. However, we have come too early, for our brothers have not yet lowered the drawbridge which the initiate must cross to reach hallowed ground. We must wait for them and therefore, if you love life, stand absolutely still. Cross your hands on your chest and keep the blindfold until the moment has come to remove it."

The candidate knows that the hour of his trial has come. He will not only need great spiritual strength and self-control, but will also have to prove that he can obey commands without hesitation. He therefore willingly obeys the orders that have been given, surrendering his fate into the hands of his supervisors.

His burning desire to know the mysteries makes him strong and powerful; he knows that the key of secrets will be his if he obeys and perseveres. Yet no matter how strong his will, he trembles on the threshold of the unknown . . . .

As he fights his first emotions and fearful presentiments in this way, standing motionless on the edge of the so-called abyss, his supervisors take two white robes, two sashes (one of gold and one of silver), and two masks (the head of a bull and the head of a lion) from a table standing in a corner. The white robe is a symbol of the magician's purity. The gold and silver sashes symbolize the Sun and Moon respectively.

In astrology, the sign of the Lion is the sign in which the Sun rules while the Moon rules the sign of the Crab, which means that the Sun and Moon influences are strongest in these signs.

The Thesmothetes are dressed in costumes that allow them to personify Pi-Ra and Pi-Ioh, the planetary spirits of Sun and Moon, to which the magicians ascribe the renewal and destruction of all earthly creatures. This symbolism also indicates that study of the law of nature is the first rung on the ladder to greater understanding. However, the meaning of this symbolism is only explained to the candidate when the tests of the first initiation are behind him.

The supervisors have barely finished putting on their costumes when a trap door opens in the ground with a fearful rumble, and a mechanical, ghostlike figure rises from it as though it has come up from an abyss and hangs suspended above the ground. At the same time the blindfold is removed from the initiate's eyes and while he is confronted with the two masked figures, the phantom passes a scythe with lightning speed in front of his face seven times, while a lugubrious voice, seemingly from the innards of the earth, menacingly warns: "Woe to the profane, who dare to disturb the peace of the dead!"

The candidate is now face to face with the three monstrous creatures who will subject him to his first test. If, despite the shock, he does not react with fright or flee from the mowing scythe, the specter disappears and the trap door clangs shut. Then the Thesmothetes remove their masks and congratulate the candidate on his courageous conduct. They say: "You have felt the cold of murderous steel and did not flinch. You have met the fearful specter and did not flee. Excellent! In your own terms, you would have earned admiration for your steadfastness. But there is a greater virtue than defying death, and that is humility. Humility triumphs over vanity and conceit. Will you also be able to conquer these in yourself?"

The candidate is reassured by the conciliatory attitude of his guides, and believing that the greatest threat is behind him, declares that he is ready for the next test. "Excellent," continue his guides. "Crawl under the altar in the eastern corner on your hands and knees. Our brothers are waiting for you to test your humility. Will you undertake this difficult journey?" The candidate declares that he is willing to try.

"Take this lamp," adds the guide. "It is the symbol of the Higher Being which follows us on our most secret paths. Go without fear! In the test of loneliness you have no one and nothing to fear but yourself." The moment the initiate receives the lamp from the hand of one of his guides, the other opens a bronze doorway by pressing a spring. At first this doorway had looked like a stylized panel in the wall, but it now reveals itself to be a doorway leading to an arched passage so low that the candidate can only go down it on his hands and knees.

The guide continues: "May this path be a foretaste of the grave for you. When the twilight of life has fallen, every person must descend into it to be freed from material ties and awaken in the world of the spirit. You have already conquered the terror of death, now conquer the terrors of the grave!"

The candidate appears to hesitate for a moment, but his guides do not seem to wish to either encourage or restrain him. They wait in total silence, pointing down the dark corridor with their right hands, demanding obedience. If, after a few minutes the candidate has not made his decision, they blindfold him and lead him out.

Any weakness in the candidate clearly appears in this test; moreover, the initiation ritual does not allow for a repetition of the test.

However, if the candidate goes freely, the guides give him the kiss of peace and wish him a good journey. As soon as he has disappeared through the opening, the bronze door closes behind him with a great rumble and a distant voice calls out: "Fools who chase knowledge and power die here!"

These chilling words, which are repeated seven times from different sources by means of clever acoustics, strike terror into the candidate.

Is he the victim of his own lack of modesty or of naive good faith? Are the magicians condemning to death in this way anyone who tries to understand their mysteries? But if this were so, why did they let him escape the whirling scythe? Why would they bury him alive? And if they have decided he must die, why have they left him the lamp?

The uncertainty is even more intolerable than the terror, and the candidate suffers terribly from this undermining vacillation. Meanwhile he moves forward, scraping his hands and knees on the sharp stones of the seemingly endless passage.

"What is to become of me if this goes on forever?" he wonders in desperation. His lamp seems to be burning out. What will he do if it goes out completely?

Laboriously he crawls on and on, his scratched hands and feet bleeding painfully, until suddenly, seemingly after hours or even years of difficult crawling he sees a light in the distance and the passage really does seem to become slightly wider and higher.

At last the tunnel of despair comes to an end in a large funnel-shaped opening with walls as smooth as polished steel. An iron ladder leads down; the lowest steps seem to disappear in the depths in the impenetrable gloom.

He now stands before the terrifying Great Unknown; to go back is impossible, for he knows that will mean certain death, but staying is not much better. In the dark he will die of hunger. It is a situation which would drive the greatest stoic insane.

Reason tells him that the only way to go in this case lies before him — he must go on until he can go no further. The ladder has seventy-eight rungs, and when he has reached the last rung he notices with a shock that it is not long enough and that there is empty space below him, and it is not possible to guess how deep it is. Suddenly a stone falls from the solid black polished marble; the time that elapses before he hears it land is so great that he realizes that the pit below him is incredibly deep. Quaking with terror — and with the last vestiges of strength at his command — he climbs up a few rungs and examines the surrounding walls with the dying light of his lamp. Suddenly he sees something which escaped his notice before: a small niche about the height of a man, and when he takes a good look at this with the lamp, he sees a corridor down which he could go. Unfortunately the ladder is on the opposite side of the niche, some distance away, so that he will have to leap over the pit to escape the yawning depths beneath him.

He will have to make this leap anyway when the lamp goes out. When finally he successfully performs this daring feat, summoning up all his strength, hope is rekindled in him. He regrets his suspicion of the magicians and now remembers their words: "Go without fear: in loneliness you have only yourself to fear."

Taking a deep breath of relief and resting on a seat in the niche hewn out of the rock, he now remembers how and why he came to be here . . .

• • •

He sees himself as a slim boy wearing his best black and white striped loincloth, entering the temple holding his father's hand and being delivered to the magicians. It was not only his father's will that brought him here; ever since he was a child he has been irresistibly attracted to this mysterious world. The pomp and splendor of religious ceremonies that appealed to most people did not mean much to him, except as an awe-inspiring spectacle. He felt that there must be more to it. His soul was filled with an unexpressed longing to worship a great and all-encompassing being; he wished to know, for he was filled with questions that he could not answer.

He had been entrusted to the care of the magicians as a novice neophyte. This status involved a fairly strict lifestyle: he was circumcised and the enjoyment of meat, fish and pulses became a thing of the past. Only occasionally was he permitted to drink some light wine.

Every morning he would sit cross-legged, serious and silent, with his fellow novices on the large terrace in front of the temple to watch the sunrise and meditate. For a certain length of time he was allowed no thoughts. He had to try and think of nothing and learn to control and study his thoughts and feelings.

After a light breakfast of vegetables and fruit he worked in the temple gardens. He knew the magicians could follow him everywhere, even when they were not present, for they had extraordinary gifts and skills incomprehensible to him. But he also knew that despite this, they were human just like him. The difference lay in their training and study, and . . . in the awfulness they had all experienced at some time in their life. His determination was absolute. He wanted to become like them, whatever the cost.

Every afternoon he sat with his fellow novices in the Great Hall. The ceiling was supported by colossal columns painted with hieroglyphics. A diffuse light hung in this enormous space where twenty-two large, wonderfully mysterious murals were painted on the walls in red, brown, black and white, eleven on either side. The novices sat here in silence for two hours every day, studying the murals and letting them sink in.

He had looked at the murals for hours, months, even years, and knew every inch by heart; they appealed to him but he could not understand their language. He saw magicians, kings, noble ladies, and he would have liked the meaning of these images to permeate him, but he lacked the key.

Slaves worked in the fields which belonged to the temple, both old and young slaves, and it was noticeable that they never left the temple grounds. The novices preparing for the Initiation were forbidden to speak with them or even to approach them.

But in the evening, when they lay on their mats, it was said that each of these slaves had once wished to become a magician, but had failed the awful test, and therefore had to serve as slaves for the rest of their lives. The young man trembled at this thought.

Once a year the Hierophant—all-knowing and all-seeing—summoned him. The Hierophant commanded respect; he was able to see what happened a long way away, and even what was going to happen in the future. Moreover, he seemed to know exactly what went on in people's minds; he saw their thoughts, moods and the state of their souls. The initiate had been called to see the Hierophant four times already and each time he had been sent away with a wave of the hand. Another year passed: meditation at sunrise, the silent study of the murals, working in the garden.

Slowly but surely the murals started to have an effect. He could feel this and unconsciously experienced the influence of these mysterious and wonderful images.

Every day he worked in the temple gardens. In the evening, the neophytes assembled together in the library, where a magician passed on knowledge and wisdom from ancient papyrus rolls—concepts to think about and words which gained in meaning as the novices meditated on them. They were emphatically told to listen to the magicians with respect; criticism was not permitted. They had to control their thoughts and feelings and were commanded only to allow those considerations which they consciously permitted themselves.

They learned to observe and empathize with life and death in nature, as though they were as one with the blossoming flowers and falling leaves. However, they did not only learn to penetrate the secret life of plants; the animal kingdom held no secrets from them either. They heard not only the plaintive cries of death, the furious roaring and howling of hunger; they also felt for the suffering creatures. In their prayers they thanked the Deity for the fullness of life and for all good gifts. They avoided harming or hurting any living creatures, which was one of the reasons why they ate no meat.

When he was summoned to the Hierophant for the fifth time, he was not sent away as before. On the contrary, the Hierophant nodded his head and spoke: "Now you may receive the Initiation, my son, and look behind the curtain. However, first we, the priests, will put you through a test which will require all your spiritual strength and powers of perseverance. This is a terrible and heavy test, but it is necessary, for only he who has enough courage and will-power, and who knows how to remain silent, can truly understand the Secrets of Life. Will, courage, and silence are qualities that are essential on the path to perfection.

"As the chance of failure is great, I must ask you, my son, do you wish to undergo this test? I am not trying to persuade you — you are still free. You can still back out and leave the temple a free man. Follow your heart when you make your decision."

Seriously and thoughtfully the initiate answered, "I wish to do it."

"Then return to your work," said the Hierophant.

In silence he bowed deeply and left the Hierophant's cell.

After three days fasting on bread and water he was led through the dark by a priest one evening. He was taken to a part of the temple that had hitherto been closed to him. They crossed passages and halls which became increasingly narrow, low, and constricted — a mysterious, threatening feeling.

In one of the long narrow spaces, a group of magicians was waiting for him. In the corner at the end of the hall there was a high old altar, with braziers on either side, containing smouldering charcoal. Fragrant incense was scattered in these, creating an intoxicating effect.

He remembered how humble he had felt, overpowered by impressions. The Hierophant, who was also present, stepped forward and asked him again, full of compassion, whether or not he had changed his mind in the meantime and decided not to undergo the tests. However, he had declared himself to be steadfast in his resolution; he wished to know and to learn.

At a sign from the Hierophant, the altar was opened. The high, narrow doors squealed open on their hinges revealing an ominous black hole.

Two Thesmothetes stepped forward. One of them took a small earthenware oil lamp from the wall while the Hierophant spoke: "These Thesmothetes will guide you to the end of the path. Take care of the lamp — you will need it — and remember: knowledge, the will, courage, and silence are not only requirements for the path to perfection. They must also be used as a guideline for saving your life. Remember that this path leads to perfection: you wish to follow that path. Excellent! You will need courage and silence. Do not forget: courage and silence. Now go, my son, go. In loneliness you have only yourself to fear."

He had hardly moved a few steps towards the altar when he heard the Hierophant add: "Once you have entered this passage, these doors will never open for you again. No one has ever used this passage as an exit. There is only *one* entrance; the exit is elsewhere.

If you lose courage on the way and give up, remember that only death or slavery awaits you; if you succeed, you will find knowledge and expertise. Now go."

Then he thought he had entered the passage with his guides, been blindfolded and led through a maze of hollow corridors. He thought he could smell the fresh evening breeze and that he stood balanced precariously on the edge of an abyss. Or had it all been an illusion, brought about by the soporific effect of the incense? He certainly remembered how abandoned he had felt when his guides handed him the lamp to assimilate the tests he had just undergone, alone.

• • •

The initiate comes out of his daydream with a jolt and disconsolately pulls himself together. Now that he has more or less recovered from his fright, he painfully gets up and, remembering the words of the Hierophant — "Will, knowledge, courage, and silence are your guideline" — decides to continue on his way.

His lamp is becoming dimmer, and just as he discovers that the niche he has found passes into a narrow passage, the lamp goes out altogether. He is filled with panic in the pitch darkness. What does he do now? There's no point thinking about it, for after all, he must go on. Feeling his way, he finally finds the entrance to the passage. He can just touch the walls on either side if he stretches out his arms. Carefully feeling the floor with his feet he stumbles through the winding passage, every moment fearing obstacles or an abyss. In the impenetrable darkness the path seems an endless path of suffering, but suddenly, when he turns a corner, a faint glow of light glimmers in the distance. With a sigh of relief he stumbles towards it. The light glows stronger and gradually he can make out the ground where he is walking.

Finally he reaches a square room with an entrance where he has just entered and an exit opposite. Behind it an infernal sea of fire rages, the flames seeming to stretch out and curl toward him with desire.

At this terrible sight his courage fails him and his whole body starts to tremble. There is no possibility of escape from this new danger — it means certain death.

He gathers up the last vestiges of his courage, for only the spiritually weak are intimidated by this sort of danger. If he were a real coward he would not be here now. The magicians have also all passed through this test and they are still alive. Admittedly he does not know how he will survive this test, but then he didn't know how he would survive the last.

The closer he gets to the fire, the more his self-confidence increases, particularly as there is no possibility of turning back. It would be better to find a quick death in the flames than to die slowly of hunger and thirst.

So he decides to run through the burning sea of fire and jumps high onto the searing flames, fearing the worst. Contrary to all expectations, nothing happens, the sea of flames turns out to be an optical illusion brought about by mirrors, and he can pass through without danger.

To be quite sure, he runs on anyway, leaving the light of the flames behind him, until he is suddenly brought to a halt when, right at his feet a dark lake yawns before him. The black surface seems to contain a riddle of unknowable depth. He hesitates, but not for long; suddenly oil spatters up around him and ignites, threatening to singe him. The fiery oven has become a reality.

Caught between a curtain of flames barring his way back, and the black water that could well contain new perils, he can only choose to go on — it is the only possibility of escape. So without a moment's hesitation, he plunges into the dark water which splashes up and is icy cold. He slips and slides down the steeply sloping floor of the lake as the water seems to be rising nearer his head with every step he takes. Only one more step and he will drown. But by the light of the fiery oven behind him he sees that he has now reached the halfway mark, and indeed, after a while it does seem as though the slope ceases to go further down and is beginning to rise.

Suddenly he notices a ladder on the other side of the lake, going up to a platform which is enclosed on three sides forming a sort of vault. In the wall in front of him he sees a closed doorway with two bronze doors between two pillars. The doors are each decorated with the head of a lion, and each head has a heavy metal ring in its mouth.

Dripping with water and shivering with cold, he laboriously climbs up the iron ladder. When he gets to the platform he notices in surprise how his footsteps seem to resound as he walks, as though he is walking on metal. He stands in front of the door and cannot go on. Looking back in despair he discovers that on the other side of the lake that he has just crossed, the reflection of the fiery oven is gradually dimming until it suddenly disappears altogether. The fire has gone out. Again darkness reigns supreme in this unknown world; the silence is full of terror and there is no sign of life. He must go on — but how?

Still shaking with cold and wet through, he feels his way forward through the dark, looking for the secret that the doorway must hold. But in vain — he cannot find any sign. Suddenly he remembers the lions' heads with the heavy rings in their mouths. They might be knockers to warn the gatekeeper that someone wants to be let in.

He decides to risk it and resolutely takes hold of the heavy rings with both hands. However, this movement seems to activate a mechanism which slides the metal floor from under his feet so that he is hanging by his hands over an abyss shrouded in darkness. He is filled with terror: this is surely the end. Desperately he clings on, but he realizes that he will not be able to hold out long. Soon he will have to let go and plunge down into the depths. Just as his hands can no longer bear his weight, the mechanism is activated again and the floor slowly slides back and falls into place.

As soon as he is back on his feet his cramped fingers let go of the iron rings which clang against the bronze doors. They slowly open for him.

He now enters a small room, with tapestries on the walls, illuminated by a copper chandelier hanging from the ceiling. In the center of this space a low sofa covered in multi-colored cushions invites him to rest.

He is received by two slaves whom he recognizes; he has seen them before in the distance working in the fields and gardens of the temple. He wishes to speak to them, but suddenly remembers the exhortation to silence. He remembers: "I've been courageous so far — more than enough. The test now could well be one of silence."

One of the slaves removes his wet loincloth, wraps him up in a warm woolen robe and urges him to rest, pointing to the sofa with his hand. The other brings in a low table, slides it next to the couch and serves a simple meal. Then they both disappear, silent and mute.

Behind the tapestries the door slowly closes. After three days of fasting and the tests he has undergone, the food tastes divine. He should really inspect the chamber but is too tired to get up. He will do it later. His only need is to rest his exhausted body.

While he stretches out on the cushions, it seems that the lighting goes slightly dimmer. But he is too tired to think about it and falls into a state of semi-sleep. One of the tapestries moves slightly aside and a long-legged, round-breasted Nubile approaches his couch; she is slim and brown, agile, and with the strength of her youth, conscious of her beauty.

She wears a thin red silk shawl with a long golden fringe around the hips. Narrow golden bangles tinkle and glitter around her upper arms and ankles. Her eyes shine, tempting and welcoming; her full red lips are an invitation which she holds a goblet of sparkling red wine in her hand.

He starts up from his reverie when she appears, and supporting himself on his arms, he looks up to take a closer look at this beautiful vision.

She laughs softly, certain of her irresistibility. Her eyes, lips and whole body are full of promises of unimaginable delights, while with her feet and hips she performs extremely controlled dance movements and her anklets tinkle gently. She comes closer and he is attracted by her stimulating fragrance. She bends over him and offers him the golden goblet.

"You have undergone the tests and have been successful. Now receive the reward you deserve, young man. Take the goblet and drink the wine; it will strengthen you and kindle love in your heart. Just as my lips desire yours, my whole body desires you. Receive, oh, receive your reward, courageous one."

She is silent. Is this really a reward, or is it another test? He hesitates.

She lays a dark hand on his shoulder. "Why don't you speak, mysterious one? Am I not pleasing to you? Say something. Speak."

The word "silence" suddenly comes to him. He desires knowledge, so he cannot speak. Roughly he pushes the girl away from him, so roughly that the goblet crashes to the floor. The spell is broken, and with a cry of fright, the temptress flees.

At that moment the curtain is drawn aside and a group of twelve Neocrores (Keepers of the Holy of Holies), dressed in white, enter through a door he has not noticed before. The leader has him blindfolded again, just as when he entered the subterranean vaults, and the procession then passes from the Sphinx through many passages to the pyramid. At various points, the doors in the passages are shut, only to be opened when the leaders have given the password and a signal of recognition.

The group of magicians is waiting for the neophyte in a crypt in the heart of the pyramid. The walls are covered in a splendid mural depicting the fifty-two spirits of the year, the seven planetary spirits and the 365 guardians of days.

Together they comprise the Golden Papyri, which contain all the teachings left the magicians by the Great Revealer of Secrets, Thoth-Hermes. All their secrets are stored here and only they are capable of deciphering them. The Hierophant initiates the neophyte into these secrets himself, but only when he has taken an oath of secrecy. The seal of wisdom is placed on the ninth and highest level.

In each corner of the crypt there is a triangular column holding respectively a marble statue of a man, a bull, a lion, and an eagle. These are the same symbols the neophyte already encountered when he was balanced on the edge of an abyss inside the Sphinx. Crowned with a soft, glowing light, these beautiful statues, together with a seven-pointed rosette on the ceiling holding seven triple oil lamps, light up the crypt.

The Hierophant, dressed in purple, is seated on a silver throne in the middle of the group of magicians, a golden crown with seven stars on his head. The other magicians, in immaculate white robes, are wearing plain gold bands on their heads and are seated on each side of the Hierophant. Behind them, under a purple canopy, there is a tall statue of the Goddess Isis — the Great Mother — as the personification of Mother Earth. This statue is composed of equal parts:

- Lead, the metal dedicated to Rempha, the Heavenly Bull ♄

- Tin — the metal dedicated to Pi-Zeous, the Rising Star ♃

- Iron — the metal dedicated to Ertosie, the Red Horus ♂

- Gold — the metal dedicated to Pi-Ra, the Heavenly Sun ☉

- Copper — the metal dedicated to Suroth, the Morning Star ♀

Mercury — the metal dedicated to Thoth-
Hermes, the Heavenly Messenger ☿

Silver — the metal dedicated to Pi-loh,
the Silver Moon ☽

Around her head Isis is wearing a triangular silver diadem with a twelve-pointed star in its center. On her breast is a golden cross with a red rosette in the center, symbolizing what has been revealed. The cross has four arms and symbolizes both infinity and the soul as manifest in the material world. Isis holds her arms stretched out in front of her body, forming a triangle with her head at the top, while with open hands and fingers outspread, she sends golden rays down to Earth. These ten rays, together with the twelve from the rosette on her forehead, depict the twenty-two secrets of the magician, which the neophyte has been studying for years without consciously understanding what it was.

In the middle of the crypt — in front of the Hierophant — there is a large silver table in the shape of a flattened hemisphere. A horoscope has been engraved in it. The signs of the zodiac are shown in a golden ring which can turn around the circumference of the tabletop, so that when the calculations have been made the signs can be moved to the correct position with mathematical precision.

The figures of the seven planetary spirits are shown in the center of the table, executed in the metal and dedicated to him. When the proper calculations have been made, these figures can also be placed in the correct position by means of magnets. The east and west points of the compass are indicated by two bronzes attached to slate tablets on which the magician makes his calculations.

The study of astrology is one of the most important subjects in which the magicians are instructed, and none of them can be admitted to a higher level if they cannot cast a horoscope in the presence of the other members of that particular level. If a magician makes a mistake in his calculations in this test, the higher levels are permanently closed to him.

Meanwhile the twelve Neocrores have led the neophyte before the Hierophant's throne. While one removes the blindfold, two others hold his arms to prevent him moving. The Hierophant speaks to him as follows:

"You once heard that we, the magicians, possessed great wisdom, and you could not rest before you had penetrated our sanctum.

"Are you satisfied now? Have you found wisdom? What has your burning desire led to? You are exhausted, dejected, imprisoned, and of your own free will you have surrendered to a group whose secrets you hope to understand, but which has shut you in the depths of the earth as a reward for your courage. You have passed our tests, but our secrets are well-guarded. Without our help you do not have the power to penetrate the core of these mysteries. You may well short-sightedly imagine that despite all the terrifying experiences, a neophyte will always manage to come through with his life and will receive wisdom as a reward for his courage.

"It probably has not occurred to you that we, the Magicians of Life and Death, could well reward such light-hearted optimism with a cruel twist. You are in our hands, and one sign would suffice to send you to be imprisoned in one of these crypts, to come to a miserable end, on bread and water.

"Yet fear not. Our wisdom leads to truth, which soon puts an end to arrogance and vanity. All we desire in return is an oath of allegiance, in which you swear to keep everything you heard or saw tonight — or will hear and see — secret. Are you prepared to take this oath?"

The neophyte, warned by one of the Neocrores, answers: "I am prepared."

The Hierophant then commands that the candidate should be taken to the altar of Isis and bids him kneel, and says: "If you are prepared, repeat the following oath after me, word for word:

> In the presence of the seven planetary spirits — executors of the Will of the Almighty, Eternal and Unchanging One — I (name of the candidate), son of (name of the father), born in (country, place, date and time of birth) swear to keep secret all I have heard and seen as well as all I will hear and see in the Holy Place of the Magicians of Life and Death. If I should ever break this oath, I deserve to be put to death as a sick jackal, my tongue will be ripped from my mouth, my heart from my body, to be buried in the sand of the sea so that the waves can carry me away to eternal oblivion.

"We will all witness your oath, and if you ever break it, an unknown avenger will follow your footsteps and find you wherever you are, even if you are on the highest throne, in order to execute the punishment you pronounced upon yourself.

"From this time, you are among the Disciples of Wisdom and you will be known to us by the title of Zelator until you deserve to be raised to a higher level because of your great application and modesty."

When the Hierophant has spoken these words, two Neocrores, each holding a cup in his hands, stand on either side of the future Zelator. Behind him, four Manlanophores (burial servants) unfold a large black cloth.

The Hierophant continues: "All magicians have made an oath of absolute allegiance to me; now in your turn, Zelator, swear an oath of unbreakable trust and obedience."

The Zelator willingly takes this oath. The Hierophant calls emphatically: "Remember that you do not make this just with your lips while lying with your heart, for untruthfulness will be punished with death."

These words are followed by an enormous clap of thunder resounding through the pyramid. Then all those present are blinded by a flash of lightning; the lights fade and the crypt is illuminated only by the flames surrounding the four statues.

The Zelator recoils in fright when he sees that the magicians surround him, pointing their swords at his heart. It is a fearsome and impressive sight. The Hierophant continues: "These swords are of the law of man, though this law seems all too often fallible, and it often happens too late, thus failing to inspire fear in those who break the law. However, we know a way which reveals the sincerity of our Zelators. Listen!

"You have just sworn absolute obedience to me. You can now prove your sincerity by accepting a test in which only your guardian can save you if he considers you worthy of living amongst us."

The magicians drop their swords and the two Neocrores walk towards him with their goblets.

Of these two goblets, the Hierophant says: "One contains a harmless drink, while the other contains a fast-acting poison. I order you to drain one of them, trusting only in your guardian."

The Zelator realizes that he must decide without hesitating. He does not have much choice, since the Neocrores still have swords in their hands. He prefers the risk of sudden death by poison than to be dishonorably struck down. Trusting to good fortune, and commending his soul to the gods, he decides, and takes the goblet offered by the Neocrores on the left, drains it in one gulp and waits anxiously for what may come.

However, if a Zelator cannot bring himself to feel this trust and refuses to carry out the order, a second peal of thunder is the sign that the Initiation is at an end.

In this case the four Melanophores will throw themselves upon him, wrap him up in the folds of the black cloth and bear him away. For anyone who hesitates to put his life in the balance for the belief to which he has just sworn allegiance twice over, is in danger of being forever unreliable because of this indecision in his spirit. He cannot be permitted to return to his former life to reveal the secrets: "I wanted to be initiated into the mysteries of the famous magicians before whom all Egypt bows down in the dust, as though they are demi-gods, but they have proved to be evil men, and no one can penetrate their mysteries unless by some miracle he can escape the chance of being poisoned or killed. I was unable to pass *one* of their tests and they punished me with contempt, but I hold them in the same contempt: they are monsters and a disgrace to the entire nation."

No, the fear or cowardice of a neophyte who has taken the oath means that he can never be freed. The magicians will not let him go, but will imprison him for seven months and give him nothing but bread and water once a day. A mute guard will serve him.

The failed Zelator is given a papyrus that contains a list of the duties which rest upon every person toward life, toward his fellow men, and above all, toward himself. Reading and thinking about this papyrus, which is an elementary catechism for initiates left by Thoth-Hermes, will serve as a consolation in his imprisonment, and will also kindle some hope in him, for the text indirectly reveals that there is a way of being freed from his imprisonment and also shows how this can come about.

After seven months of confinement, he is offered the goblets once more. If the initiate succeeds in draining one this time, he regains his freedom. However, he will never be permitted to work at higher levels; he will always retain the title of Zelator. However, if he refuses again, the process is repeated until he empties one of the goblets — if death has not already put an end to his silent imprisonment. However, if he immediately accepts and drains the goblet, as in the initiation we describe, the Hierophant wastes no time in telling the Zelator before him that really he was in no danger, and that both cups contained only wine mixed with a slow dream-evoking drug.

Meawhile the young Zelator listens to the words which the Hierophant speaks after praising him for his courage and trust:

"Magic consists of two elements, knowledge and strength. Without knowledge, strength is not perfect; and without strength, no one can achieve anything which is worth achieving. Know how to suffer so as to remain unaffected by suffering. Know how to die so as to embrace immortality; know how to do away with the acquisition of possessions. These are the three main secrets of your new life for which we have prepared you by means of these tests.

"The magician is a priest serving truth — in other words the guardian of its mysteries and the possessor of its strength. However, there are very few young magicians who are able to understand the consequences of their status. To begin with, you will have to learn to control your senses so that your spirit can be free. You will be rewarded with a clear insight if you successfully do this.

"The strongest among us attain the level of *Prophet* or *Theurg*. The former sees the causes and consequences of the past for the present through the past, and can therefore predict the inevitable future. The latter seems to perform miracles because of his knowledge of natural laws which are still unknown to us. He knows the hidden motives existing behind what we call Life, the consequences of these for the present, as well as the future. You, too, will be able to reach the level of "Prophet" or "Theurg" if you are prepared to work for seven years in silence and loneliness and to achieve what is possible for human understanding in all those fields.

"Pursue your career with the same dedication that you started with, and may the Great Mother, the Exalted Goddess Isis, inspire you.

"However, if you remain among us to complete your studies and fulfill the duties which will be laid upon you if you are considered worthy of them, or if you go away to pass on the teachings elsewhere, always remember the oath which binds you to us. In order that it will never be erased from your memory, I request you to witness the performance of a judgment that is promised to those deserving of it."

After these words, the procession continues to the inner sanctum. Everyone takes his place in a semicircle around the Hierophant, who stands before the altar armed with a sword and scepter.

With his arms crossed he calls out, breaking the total silence: "My sons, what time is it?" and as one the magicians answers: "The hour of the law!" seven regular crashes issue from the bowels of the earth.

The Hierophant continues: "Where the hour of the law has come, I order that justice proceed."

At the foot of the altar, a trapdoor opens with a loud crash, and all sorts of sounds come up from the depths—first the dragging of chains, followed by the noise of a skirmish, then raging, and a human voice calling for mercy in heart-rending death throes, then . . . nothing, the silence of the grave . . .

After a short pause, the Hierophant says: "That is the death of those who have committed perjury. Justice has been done on those who deserve it. Go, see, and be convinced!"

The Zelator descends into the square hole, surrounded by twelve Neocrores, and by the flickering light of the lamp he sees how a Sphinx is tearing apart a human body with his claws. He wants to turn back and flee from this nightmare, but the Neocrores who are standing behind him restrain him. However, as soon as he recovers from his panic and regains his composure, the terrible vision has disappeared.

This macabre event makes an irradicable impression on the Zelator, though he will never be sure whether what he saw was a dream, a vision, a hallucination, or reality. Then the procession returns to the Hierophant.

"Come!" says the Hierophant, taking the young Zelator by the hand and turning to the others, "follow us." They form a line in pairs behind him and follow him chanting the ancient refrain:

> Praise Osiris, the Glorious Sun,
> Creator of Worlds,
> The Path through Time . . .

Thus the procession wends its way through passages, temples and gardens until it enters a small hall with a large round window in the ceiling. The window is open, and the full moon shines in, bathing the pond in the middle of the hall in its magic light.

The High Priest now intones: "Today a new life is starting for you. You have had some impressive and shocking experiences which you will never be able to forget. Today your life is divided into two parts: innocent youth lies behind you; before you a path leads upwards, full of light. You have not learned anything new today, but it has proved that you have courage, and silence, and can control your senses. However, what you will learn here will make you a person who will act with knowledge from this day up to your death and afterwards.

"Enter the pond, my son, and perform the Holy Ablutions so that you may be reborn."

The young priest obeys.

"Consider this water as the grave of your past that you are throwing off as you enter the water. Understand when you leave it that death is not an end, and that the grave will merely receive your body. Immerse yourself; leave your cloak and loincloth in the water as a sign that only your cocoon is left behind."

The young priest obeys and walks naked to the edge.

"Dress him in the white cloak of the Priests of Osiris," the High Priest continues. "You have trodden the path, but you are at the very beginning and it is a long way. You will not have to undergo any more tests, but there is still much to learn before you have completed the great journey of the Initiation. Now go and rest and return tomorrow morning before sunrise to the great hall for morning exercises."

The High Priest disappears and one of the magicians steps towards the young priest and says: "Come, I will show you where you are to live."

In silence the magician leads the newcomer outside through various passages and halls. In the moonlight he sees a beautiful garden. In the middle there is a stream with gravel on either side, and the slow-running water feeds several ponds covered with lotus flowers and water lilies.

The palm trees on the banks of the ponds tower above a number of small, flat-roofed houses hidden between the shrubs and flowers in a green world, protecting them with their long shadows. The whole complex is surrounded by a high wall.

The young priest looks around. "I've never been here," he says.

"These are the houses of the unmarried priests. Neophytes cannot enter this garden."

"Who looks after all this?" he asks, pointing at the beautiful flowerbeds.

"Slaves."

"Are they bought for the temple?"

"No, that's not necessary."

"Why not?"

"Those who do not pass the last test and lose themselves in sensual pleasure do not lose their life, but they do surrender their freedom. They may never leave the holy temple grounds on pain of death. So . . . if you had not rejected the Nubian today, you would have been a slave now."

"But what about the Nubian?"

"We buy female slaves, but if she succeeds in tempting a neophyte, she regains her freedom. . . . She knows that and therefore does her very best."

Silently the young priest thanks his lucky stars and asks: "But suppose I had not been able to find my way out of the well."

"We've taken more than one body out of it."

"Isn't that inhuman?"

"We don't force anyone to become a priest of Osiris. You, too, had a choice — you could have gone back. However, the altar gates are no longer open to those who give up. Only a few years ago, a neophyte who did not dare to go into the abyss died of starvation under the altar . . . . But enough of this. Here is your home," said the priest and pointed at a small white plaster house, dwarfed by a few magnificent palm trees.

"You can receive family and friends in the forecourt of the temple. Only the priests and their servants may enter here. Your family will be overjoyed to see you in your priest's raiments. And now, good night. I will come and fetch you before sunrise to take you to the High Priest."

The young priest sank down on the bed. The cool night air came in through the window and he covered himself up. Frogs croaked in the ponds under the lotus flowers. Exhausted with the shocking events he had experienced, he succumbed to a well-deserved sleep full of wonderful, colorful dreams.

Next morning he joins the other priests in the sacred library. Shortly before sunrise they proceed outside in pairs and stand still before two colossal statues in a position of meditation, their hands on their knees. The procession waits for the sun to rise, and as soon as it has appeared behind the mountains, lighting up the yellow sand of the desert, the priests fall to their knees and bend their heads down to the earth. When the rays of the sun touch the lips of the statues, a high, clear, ringing sound can be heard, like the vibrating of a taut wire.

The priests stand up. The High Priest turns to the Zelator: "You are one of us," he says, "but we have all received confirmation of our priesthood from the mouths of these stone statues. Once again we have asked the Gods to complete the work that you have begun, and the dead stone will answer you, Sun Child, just as it has answered the morning greeting of the sun with its clear ringing tone."

The priests form a semi-circle around the statues and rhythmically begin to sing. They begin in the key of C, the first note of the scale:

> Osiris, Osiris
> Mighty Lord,
> Give a sign
> To Your Suppliant Son!

In D, the second note of the scale, they sing:

> Isis, Isis
> Blessed Mother,
> Give a sign
> To Your Suppliant Son!

In E, the third note of the scale, they sing:

> Horus, Horus,
> Spirit of the Gods,
> Give an answer
> To the suppliant pilgrim.

In F, the fourth note of the scale, they sing:

> He who obeys all laws
> In his readiness to follow!

In G, the fifth note of the scale, they sing:

> He who fears and honors
> The Gods
> And himself desires
> Deification

Then they sing in A, the sixth note of the scale:

> Which comes from Love
> And awakens as Love
> So that Love
> Becomes Truth.

Finally they all sing together in the seventh note, B:

> Osiris and Isis
> And Horus, Oh thou Three
> We beg you on our knees
> That if the Sun Child
> Who is here now
> Is welcomed as your son
> Then let this dead stone
> Ring with a sacred tone.

When the priests have finished singing the seventh note, the same clear sound is heard from the lips of the statue as that which was heard at sunrise.

The High Priest says: "Blessed are you, my son; even the stones must speak and let you know that you have pleased the Gods."

The priests return to the library, singing a hymn, and slowly the white procession dissolves in the dark doorway of the temple.

Part Two

THE SECRETS

The First Symbol

The next day just before sunrise, a young priest came to fetch the newcomer and took him to a gallery with twenty-two columns covered in hieroglyphs which supported the roof, eleven on the left and eleven on the right. The mysterious paintings and symbols immediately showed him that this was the hall where he had spent so many years. The images were illuminated by eleven onyx sphinxes standing on tripods and filled with fragrant oil that was burning brightly. It all made a great impression on him.

The High Priest addressed him as follows, after a greeting of welcome: "These pictures contain, in symbolic form, everything we know. Everything the Gods wished to reveal, everything we mortals can understand, is contained in them.

Figure 1. The seven symbols of Osiris.

"These pictures, which we call the *Book of Thoth*, and which reflect a summary of the forty Books of Thoth, the God of Wisdom, tell of the essence of the God we serve, of the world and its creation, and the path humanity will follow. In this way they reveal the natural laws to which art, society, science and the entire universe are subject.

"They contain infinitely more than you can imagine at this time. However, I will give you the key to enable you to read this Book.

"In future you will spend many hours here to gain knowledge and insight from these symbols. At the appropriate time I will also tell you more about the relationship between these paintings. However, today I merely want you to realize what you can read about yourself in this wonderful book. Your entire development — in all your material lives, and through countless centuries which you spent in the spiritual realms — can be found here, for you came from the lap of the Higher Being and you will return there.

"Thought is the beginning of all things; everything was created from Divine Thought.

"Observe the first symbol. It represents the greatest God, the Infinite, Eternal, Unnameable, Absolute Active, never totally understood. It is not a representation of Osiris, but a symbolic revelation of his Essence. You see a man in the raiment of a magician who knows and controls the eternal laws of nature, one who knows.

"Look at the position of his hands: he commands in Heaven and makes things real on Earth. Thus he is a summary of the great primitive principle, of the Creator, by whom all things were created and to whom all things will return, whose hand reaches everywhere, whose eyes see everything, whose ears hear everything, who is omnipotent and omnipresent. He is also the Great Lawgiver who, in his wisdom, made the laws which allowed the Creation to take place and continue. Mankind, the elements and natural forces, all life and all death are ruled by him. In front of him on the table there are four symbols: a Staff, a Goblet, a Sword and a Coin. They are symbols with many meanings. For today, it will suffice if I tell you that they represent the human body and human society in various images.

"The Staff represents the brain which produces thoughts; the Goblet stands for the breathing breast which allows us to live; the Sword, which can change the circumstances of life, points to the stomach, which digests the food that is eaten. The Coin, the money that passes from hand to hand, represents the sexual organs and the creation of new generations.

"At the social level, the Staff represents those who testify to society — the poets, artists and inventors. The Goblets show us the preservers — judges, scholars, collectors. The Swords reveal those who reorganize, who are eager to fight, who strive for change and who change the form and values of society. The Coins represent the pregnant and productive members of society — the people who have many children and from which higher classes develop. Osiris is the Great One, who produces infinite series of numbers but is not descended from anyone himself. You come from him; your spirit, the core of your personality is a spark of the primeval fire, a drop of the primeval sea and it is His will that you go through life along the great curve, up and down, back to him in a large circle — a snake eating its own tail.

"Your spirit has a divine origin and has all the characteristics of the Higher Being, just as a drop has all the characteristics of the primeval sea surrounding the Earth. But your spirit is not yet active, it sleeps while you must develop into a ruler. It is your body and its needs, and not the soul and its longings, that must be the decisive factor for you. Your spirit is that which makes you a Child of God.

"There is only one Creator and his children are part of him. They are the conscious. Therefore listen: men are immortal gods and the gods were immortal men. That is the goal to which you must aspire from this day forth.

"Now go in peace and return tomorrow morning early."

The Second Symbol

The second day the Hierophant spoke the following words: "The first mural showed you your origin and your goal, what you will become. The questions where do we come from, where are we going, are answered in this first mural in broad terms. Today you will see the second image: Isis, the Great Mother.

"The One has divided into two and created Two. The Female is added to the Male, or in other words, the female element has separated away from the male. This symbol is called the Priestess — Absolute Passivity. It shows you the first step on the path you trod yesterday.

"You see a royal lady sitting on a throne in front of a curtain, holding two keys in her left hand and a papyrus scroll in her right hand. She says to you: 'If

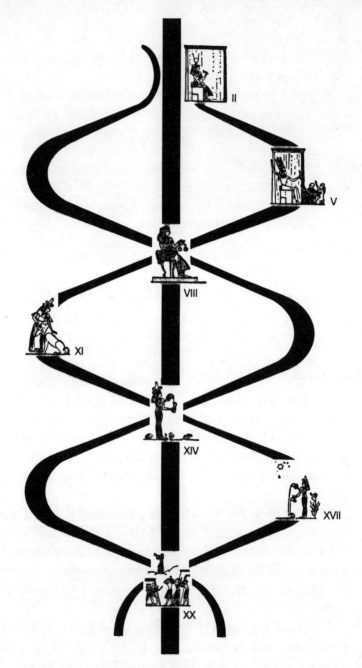

Figure 2. The seven symbols of Isis.

you wish to know what is behind the curtain, if you wish to learn about those areas which are still invisible to you and to develop your latent skills, you must first study the papyri and above all the *Book of Thoth*. Then, when the time is right, I will open the door leading to these areas with the keys I hold in my hand, and before death you will be able to enter both the Realm of Torture and the Realm of Eternal Joy.

'You will see the Great Law of Sowing and Harvesting, for everything we do is sowing, and all our experiences and adventures are harvests. You will be able to convince yourself that all that is visible merely expresses the invisible and is also based on this. Just as the temple first existed in the creative imagination of the architect before it was built, the universe first existed in the mind of the Creator before matter was imbued with life.'

"Let the contents of the sacred texts enter your spirit and create a place in yourself for new and deeper thoughts.

"Now go, learn and understand!"

The Third Symbol

On the third day the Hierophant stood before the third image and spoke: "This mural, my son, represents the God Horus, the Eagle, the Spirit. It does not merely depict the well-known image of a man with the head of a sparrow hawk. It shows his essence, represented symbolically. Horus is considered to be the son of Isis and Osiris. This mural is called the Queen. She rules!

"You will see, she has a scepter in her hand and wears a star-studded crown on her head. A colorful carpet of spring meadow blossoms is at her feet, for she rules the earth — as shown by her garland of flowers. The eagle and the stars on her crown mean that she also governs the universe. The Queen who reigns over All is Nature, the life force that penetrates everywhere, the absolute Neuter, the Spirit. Everything was created

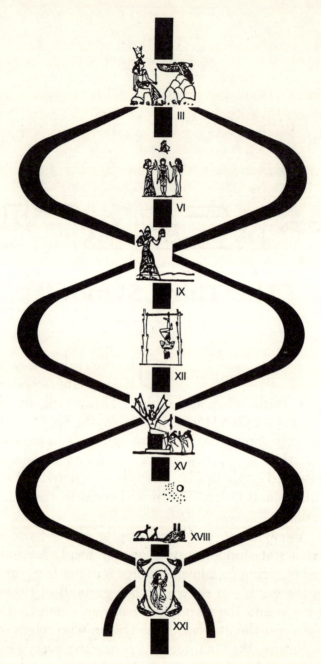

Figure 3. The seven symbols of Horus.

from the thoughts of the primeval spirit, just as the words we speak and our visible actions spring from our thoughts. However, in our thoughts the same spirit rules as in words and deeds.

"Therefore see before you the trinty: Osiris—thought; Isis—the word; and Horus—the spirit. Be filled with him, become equal to him, obey him and he will bear you up on his eagles' wings toward your goal—perfection.

"Observe the eagle on the rocks next to the Queen. She represents an unfulfilled promise. He is still resting, but is ready to spread his mighty wings, and if you trust yourself to him, he will soar up toward the sun with you. His word is up, high above us, not forward as is often assumed by those for whom going onward is actually a step backward; for the All develops upward in great turning spirals, and anything that opposes this upward movement is destroyed.

"My son, the Universe originates from two tremendous forces which touch, cross, and join together without becoming confused, without losing their own character, without losing sight of their goal. These are the Force of the Spirit and the Wave of Life. The Force of the Spirit originates from the heart of God; each spark—the human spirit—must descend into matter, assume a material form and then conquer this so that it can continue to develop as a result of this fight. In the Kingdom of Death they cleanse themselves of impurities they have acquired and rise, purified, up to the Kingdom of Life. They stay there until they are once again dragged down by matter: in reincarnation in matter they gain greater maturity through new experiences, and gain new strength by overcoming difficulties. In this way spirits rise and descend, but always in the ever higher circles of the divine spiral. The higher they go, the more love they radiate, and they exude so much warmth that all selfishness burns away until they finally reach the top. Burning with love, they unite with the primeval fire—the so-called Great Leap.

"By descending into matter, the spirits are not only forced to develop themselves, but they also exert an ennobling influence on the material form in which they are temporarily accommodated. These material forms are actually manifestations of the Great Wave of Life, which is also constantly developing higher forms of life.

"The Wave of Life originates in the lap of the God and permeates space and time. The mineral world is created over thousands of years, from deposits of air and water, from myriads of invisibly small impurities. Slowly life moves through this heavy matter, and in the core of the earth crystals form, while on the surface the primeval rocks are weathered. On these weathered rocks, mosses and ferns will grow.

"The rocks continue to weather and the vegetation becomes increasingly luxuriant. Animal life now also developed, from the lowest to the highest forms. Thus the Wave of Life passes through the animal and plant kingdoms, as well as that of man and the spirit, creating new and consistently higher forms until it also returns to the lap of God. These two spirals, the Force of the Spirit and the Force of Life, which exist side by side, together promote the evolution of the universe.

"However, my son, there is a shorter, steeper path for reaching the top than this natural path, and that is through Initiation. You can attain the highest point by following a path that gradually ascends—but you can also climb more quickly up a steep, narrow and extremely difficult path.

"There are spirits which are driven to take the path of Initiation. These are the chosen who wish to attain the goal faster so that they can help others onward. They lead a difficult life, full of sadness and problems, but it is also rich in insight and silent joy. In one lifetime, they experience the content of many lives, for they wish to go on, even at that price. These chosen ones have been called by the gods. They are the ones who wish to know, who seek the answer to the question: "Where do we come from and where are we going?" They are prepared to subject themselves to tests and undergo trials—and you are one of them. They reach maturity sooner than others, and will find peace and joy even in this life through giving help, support, comfort, service, care and love.

"This is your path. Now go and thank the Gods."

The Fourth Symbol

On the fourth day the High Priest spoke these words: "You are now standing, my son, before a mural known as the *Pharaoh*. In the first mural, you saw the creative Deity commanding the elements, and now, in this fourth one, you see the God who governs Creation — the Cube — by means of fixed laws.

"Laws govern the Universe. No one can escape these laws. The two crowns on the head of the Pharaoh, and the two scepters in his hands, reveal that with these laws he governs both the world that is visible and those that are still invisible to us.

"The universe which he governs is represented by a cube or die, for the Law of Fours is the basic Law of Creation; everything depends on the fourfold law. The Deity is a trinity: Osiris, Isis and Horus. The eternal primaeval beginning, the Active Principle, breaks away part of itself; the Passive Principle receives this part. In this way, a relationship is created between these two principles: the third, which develops from this, is not only the result but also the connection. That is why Deity is always represented by a triangle.

"However, if this Deity, existing at a spiritual level, wishes to create a Universe with thousands of solar systems and millions of stars, the visible world is a fourth part. If a straight line is added to an opening triangle, this forms a square. That is why the Universe, the Cosmos, is represented by a square. And this mysterious Law of Fours does seem to dominate everywhere. There are four points of the compass: north, south, east and west; the universe consists of four elements. There are four seasons and the day is divided into four parts. We go from the cradle to the grave in four stages: child, youth, adult, greybeard. And you, my son, are composed of four parts, if you consider yourself carefully — body, life, spirit and self.

"You have a material body and a life that shines softly for a seer, which penetrates and glows around the material body. After death these bodies dissolve in the impurities from which they were created. For death is merely a loosening of the ties which bind together the four parts of which we are made up.

"Your spiritual body, the third part, which consists of a very fine material to which the impurities of the material body adhere, leaves a visible shell after death, at the same time as the Self, the divine spark, the fourth part. Then it passes through the realm of Shadows and Death. As you see, the number four is a dominant factor, also regarding the way in which we are composed.

"Last of all, we will observe the position of the Pharaoh, the Law, the Will. It reveals yet another great truth expressed symbolically: 'the Deity rules over his creation.' Note the position of the arms. Together with the head, they form a triangle, and the legs crossed together form a square. This can only be interpreted in one way: 'the Deity rules over the universe.'

"When you observe the universe and wish to understand more of the essence of God, you must first learn the laws with which Deity rules over the Universe. The laws of God are the first thing the seeker will find on his way to truth.

"Now go in peace and let all this resonate in you."

The Fifth Symbol

On the fifth day the High Priest spoke thus: "My son, you are now standing before an image which bears my name. It is called High Priest and signifies authority, intelligence, verbal instruction and whispered information.

"You can see the High Priest sitting in front of the curtain, like the Priestess in the second mural. This means that there is a relationship between the two. There is truly such a relationship, for both indicate the importance of receiving instruction. However, note the difference: the papyrus in the Priestess' hand advised you to find wisdom and insight in scrolls and books. This mural does not depict a scroll or book in the master's hand; his raised hand points up, indicating a higher form of instruction—the familiar spoken teaching which you are now receiving from me. This is shown not only by the profound, all-embracing symbols that you see before you, but also from remarks about hidden knowledge of the invisible world, concealed behind the curtain. The purpose of this teaching is shown on both murals — both in the second and the fifth symbol; the curtain and the two keys represent the revelation of the two great kingdoms behind the curtain — behind appearances.

"However, it is important and useful to enter these realms and know them, for knowledge of the great plan will enable you to communicate with higher beings. In this way, you will actually be able to participate in the evolution of the universe.

"There are things which cannot be shown to everyone at all times, but can only be passed on at the right time to those who are prepared. The hour has now come for you. I shall give you a word, mention a name, give you a key, so you can enter these invisible worlds."

The High Priest bent down over the young Zelator and whispered a name of five syllables in his ear.

"Did you understand?"

"Yes."

"Repeat the word. Whisper it in my ear."

The young priest did so.

"Very good, my son. Do not forget the word, but never speak it lightly, for this could have terrible consequences for you. It is the beginning of all things which you do not yet know.

"Tonight, and for the next four nights, when you have performed your last meditation, you must stretch out on your bed and speak the word I have given you out loud. This word has supernatural powers, and conjures up a spirit which belongs in spheres above us, and which has been commanded by still higher spirits to supervise your development. In the course of the next five nights it will reveal itself to you.

"Always remember your guiding principles: knowledge, will, courage, silence.

"There is another difference between the two murals. The Priestess does not have any pupils around her to listen to her, or with hands raised, asking for instruction. Pupils are those who wish to learn and who gather at the feet of a teacher — as you have come to me — but their motives are often very different. This reveals the distinction between white and black magic, which is shown by the difference in dress. Both paths are depicted. The pupil wearing white has honest intentions; he is holding his right hand on his heart. His motives are pure because he has been driven to God by his desire to know, and in this way to acquire insight into the plans of God. He wishes to help, to serve and be useful.

"The pupil in the black cloak is quite different. He, too, desires knowledge, but his reasons are impure, for he seeks knowledge and power for his own ends. His heart is filled with greed for money and lust, and therefore he will be overcome by his selfishness. However, you must stay on the path of love and light, and avoid that slippery path of selfishness and darkness.

"Now go in peace, and thank the gods who have chosen you."

• • •

All day the young priest thought of the evening to come. In his mind, he repeated the five syllable word over and over. The sun set and the Zelator meditated on his mat; he could not concentrate. His thoughts constantly reached for the mysterious word. When he had finished his exercises, he stretched out on his bed. The sickle-shaped waning moon shone through the window. Knowledge, will, courage. He spoke the word out loud and waited for what was to come.

Suddenly he was overcome by panic, paralyzed spiritually and physically, feeling something invisible and supernatural present around him. For a moment it hung around him threateningly, and then, as suddenly as it had come, it disappeared. He breathed a sigh of relief, commended himself to the protection of the Gods, and fell into a deep sleep.

The Sixth Symbol

On the sixth day the High Priest spoke thus: "The sixth mural, which represents beauty and love, depicts a young man standing undecidedly between two women; he must choose. It is the spirit of the third mural that forces the chosen one to make this choice. The woman on the right represents wisdom; the one on the left, naked with flowers in her hair, represents sensuality.

"He is observed, as we all are. In the clouds you see an angel aiming the arrow in his bow at a place between the young man and the naked woman. If the young man chooses the transient pleasure of the senses, he will be painfully punished by higher powers for his own good, so he can change his mind and return to the path after straying off it.

"On the day when you underwent your test, my son, you chose wisdom, which grants quiet joy.

However, you are not at the end of all the tests. Admittedly, we will not subject you to any more physical tests, but the desire to reproduce, which the Gods have given us, will constantly recur in you. There are also creatures that are still invisible to us, spirits from a lower level which enjoy human sensuality, and who feed on the seed and blood that has been spilt and engender lascivious thoughts in mortals to stimulate them. This is why it is so important to control your thoughts and be able to reject impure impulses.

"The strength of the reproductive urge is a blessing when it follows the proper path and is kept in hand. This strength has not only been given us in order to gratify passing sensual desire, but also to produce a healthy offspring, for mankind must procreate and develop. However, it accords even more with the will of God when this energy is used at an intellectual level by means of spiritual activity and concentration. Through this sort of effort some of the members of our society will succeed in achieving a higher level, enabling others to go further.

"Now go in peace."

• • •

That evening the young priest again pronounced the mysterious word when he laid himself down to rest, and waited. Once again he was overcome by a feeling of deep horror. In the clear moonlight he saw a vague shape — a sort of pillar, or cloud, at the entrance to his room.

The shape stood still. The young priest could not say a word and stared at the apparition in amazement. The shape disappeared without a sound, just as it had come.

The Seventh Symbol

On the seventh day the High Priest spoke thus: "Every symbol develops from another. Hidden paths run across the *Book of Thoth*. For example, there is a magic path which is related to the interrelation of numbers.

"Today, we will show you more of the path of Osiris. The symbol before you now shows you the activities of Osiris. His influence can be discerned from the first to the nineteenth symbol, always leaving out two symbols. Thus he covers the images I, IV, VII, X, XIII, XVI and XIX; in other words, seven symbols.

"The first thing we mortals will notice about this God, who treads such high levels that he is impenetrable and inaccessible to most people, is the existence of certain laws (Symbol IV). However, laws evoke authority (Symbol V) so that the Divine Plan can be achieved (Symbol VII).

"My son, you have been called to perfection in the Divine Plan. This means not only that you must destroy all that is bad and unworthy in yourself, and that you must develop higher and more refined skills, but also that you should seek insight into the broad lines of God's policy. Let us now take a closer look at today's mural. It can lead to all sorts of conclusions which provide a wealth of food for thought.

"The chariot of Osiris (symbol VII) represents the realization of the Great Plan. It shows a man standing up and driving a chariot. The crown on his head and the scepter in his hand reveal a relationship with the Pharoah (symbol IV).

"Symbol I showed God, who created the universe. Symbol IV showed the Deity resting after the creation and governing the world he had created with his laws. Symbol VII shows God leading his creation toward perfection.

"The stars on the canopy of the chariot indicate that myriads of constellations are also involved in evolution. The winged disc also painted on the chariot means that Earth, like the rest of the universe, is moving toward ever-higher stages of development. The phallus on the front of the chariot reveals that generation follows generation, always improving, and the forms in which the spirit is embodied are becoming increasingly complete by means of education and instruction. Also note the scepter in the hand of the chariot driver. It consists of a triangle inside a circle surrounded by a square, which means: 'God is inside his creation for all eternity.' The Eternal One is faithful. He will never abandon the work of his hands. Learn to find peace and trust in this certainty.

"The black and white sphinxes pulling the chariot represent the forces of good and evil, which, in serving the Deity, contribute to the realization of the Great Plan. The sphinx is an enigmatic creature; at times it is incomprehensible how the Divine Plan can be served by certain events. We must not allow this either to excite us or irritate us, but learn to accept it with complete trust. After all, it would not be difficult for him to destroy evil with it, would it? However, this will never happen because, apart from the fact that this would disturb the equilibrium, evil is essential for the instruction of the children of God. They must be able to encounter dissolution if the choice between good and evil is to be as meaningful as possible. They must be prepared to fight evil, and in order to acquire physical strength, they must practice. For if the black sphinx pulls the chariot harder, the white one will also have to accelerate. Everything serves the great plan, for everything comes from Deity. He maintains everything and everything returns to him.

"Now go and find peace in this knowledge . . . ."

• • •

That evening the young priest again spoke the mysterious word out loud. He was aware of only a slight fearfulness.

After a few moments the cloud appeared. It split in two and a large man in a grey robe appeared in the opening of the door. A muted light shone through his robes. Again the young priest could not speak a word.

The Eighth Symbol

On the eighth day the High Priest spoke thus: "The symbol we will study today stands for trust and justice. Just as Symbol VII is linked with Symbols I and IV, Symbol VIII is related to Symbols II and V. Symbols II and VI promised that what lies behind the curtain would be revealed. Symbol VIII (truth and justice) now reveals the essence of that which lies behind this curtain, namely truth.

"You do not have to learn the various conflicting systems of the philosophers. Nor do you have to bow down in humility before the teachings of any temples. When you have made a careful assessment you can recognize what is real and true. You are now on the Isis path, which runs through Symbols II, V, VIII, IX, XIV, XVII and XX of the *Book of Thoth*.

"Written and verbal instruction can lead you to recognize the truth and show you the laws of sowing and reaping, sound and resonance, action and reaction. Allow Symbol VIII to thoroughly permeate you. The Queen, sitting on a throne, blindfolded, holds a sword and a pair of scales in her hands. Sitting reveals peace and equilibrium.

"Her blindfolded eyes show that judgment takes place impartially, out of sight of the person concerned. She cannot be influenced by beauty or bribed by riches. She is just in her assessment and punishment. However, if she asks: 'How do I know whether my insight and my experiences are really true?' the following symbol on the Isis path, the eleventh symbol, gives the answer: 'Courage and magical power.'

"They are the test of knowing whether you really have found truth, for only truth and knowledge produce courage. In the first place, you will have courage to approach death; not the courage of the brave man who bites his lips and looks in the face of death with a strong will, but the courage of the wise man who knows that death is an event often repeated, a transition and not an end.

"However, you shall not only have courage in the face of death, but also in the face of suffering and in defending your opinion. You will be able to tolerate suffering with equanimity because you are aware of its transience, so it does not inspire you with fear. Truth protects you from fear, for you have nothing to fear: everything, both suffering and joy, brings you nearer your goal — perfection.

"That is the first characteristic of truth. The other is that you will discover and develop capacities within yourself that you did not know existed. Just as the stars tranquilly follow their orbits in space, so you will grow towards your goal in harmony with the rhythm of the cosmos. Your equilibrium and peace will be great, for you will discover the justice of the Great Law in everything and everyone. You will be able to follow the invisible thread from human to human, from life to life. Your equilibrium will be unshakeable and your joy unclouded.

"Now go and thank the gods."

• • •

The young priest awaited the evening impatiently and without fear. He had understood that the being from higher spheres wished to accustom him to his presence gradually, so that he could cope with his appearance.

After his meditation he stretched out on his bed and spoke the word out loud. The moon shone. He waited. Then he heard music of unknown, unimaginable beauty, and saw the cloud gradually dissolve to be replaced by a luminous figure in white.

A serious, awe-inspiring man spoke as follows: "I am the spirit who accompanies you from birth to the grave, from life to life."

Although the man spoke, the young priest did not hear a voice. He was only aware of the voice inside himself and was unable to ask any questions. He wanted to ask questions but could not.

"Tomorrow you will be able to speak."

The spirit had disappeared.

The Ninth Symbol

On the ninth day the High Priest spoke thus: "Today we will follow the path of Horus which runs through Symbols II, VI, IX, XII, XV, XVIII and XXI of the *Book of Thoth*. It is a path of suffering, although it leads to great heights.

"Look carefully at the ninth symbol, the third stage of the path of Horus: the man you see there is called the Pilgrim. You will note four things about him: his pilgrimage leads him through the desert; he wears a hood on his head; he holds a staff in one hand; in his other hand he has a lantern.

"First: his pilgrimage through the desert. He has understood the relative nature of things and now feels the need to master characteristics and skills which are timeless.

"He feels uprooted, because he is aware of the realm of light and life. He is on his guard and moves carefully: he does not feel at home, even when he is traveling. And you, my son, you, too, are not at home in this country, on this earth.

"Your spirit is at home in the realm of light and life, whence you came, and whither you will return after each time you are embodied as a human being. A spirit often has the experience of walking around as though in a desert. It longs to be where it is not bound to the body, no longer tempted by lust, or limited by time and space. This is why the man who is ruled by a spirit is a pilgrim in life. He is merely passing through.

"Secondly: the hood. This, too, has a deeper significance. The hood means that he cannot look left or right; he can only look straight ahead. The same applies for a person who has become aware of his vocation. He does not worry about his former life, or about family traditions, nor does he long for pleasures which he could enjoy, but which would inhibit his development. No, he looks ahead and up. He is irresistibly attracted by the radiant heights in the distance. He wishes to become what he has been chosen to be; he strives to conquer so that he can pass this on to others.

"Thirdly, the staff. This symbolizes the contents of the Sacred Books. The pilgrim gains support from what he learns from these. The miraculous wisdom which he found there, the irrefutable logic of their structure constantly keep his feet firmly on the ground. He needs this support, for although he is a pilgrim, he is apparently a creature composed of contradictions. Not only the voice of the spirit can be heard; there are also the passions and needs of the body and the subtler longings of the soul also make themselves heard, not to mention everything that can influence him and which could shake his steadfast purpose. He truly needs the staff to remain firm and steady. The memory of the great evolution of all things helps him to see certain thoughts, temptations and concerns in the light of eternity, and thereby conquer conflicting tendencies. The thought that his staff might change into a royal scepter at the end of his pilgrimage gives the pilgrim such special strength that he stays upright.

"Finally, and fourthly, the lantern. A shielded light familiar to him and insight given him by beings from higher spheres light up the pilgrim's path, showing him the stones, holes, and snakes so he can avoid them. The lantern does not light up the whole path, merely part of it. If the pilgrim were able to see it all, his courage might fail him when he saw all the difficulties and tests; this is why the path is only revealed to him step by step.

"Now go in peace, my son, and let what you have heard resonate in you."

• • •

The young priest entered his room solemnly, deep in thought. It was a stormy evening. Great banks of clouds passed in front of the moon, and the tall palm trees in the garden bent down under the weight of the wind blowing through their crowns.

The young priest lay down and gathered his courage, for there were many questions he wished to ask. He spoke the mysterious word.

Before long, the sky again filled with charming sounds of singing, while at the same time a subtle fragrance entered the room. The cloud passed through the door, split into two, and the Leader appeared in a long garment and shining with inner light. He radiated nobility and his presence commanded respect.

He approached the young priest. The young man remembered that there were many questions he wished to ask the Leader, but his memory failed him; he had forgotten them.

He could only feel the presence of this exalted inhabitant of higher spheres. Again he heard a voice within him: "Tomorrow is the day when you will pass from knowledge into insight. Tomorrow I will lead you into the realm of shadows and eternal life, the world of real existence."

The young priest wished to ask questions but he was speechless. Then suddenly he felt one question spring to his lips: "If I have been on earth in an earlier life and spent the time in between in invisible spheres, why do I not remember this?"

"Because there are boundaries between the different realms, veiled in such a way that they cover the consciousness of mortals when they move from one realm to another. It is as though we drink from a stream of oblivion, but you will learn to lift the veils and to remember in one realm what you have seen and done in others."

The young priest wished to ask many more questions, but nothing sprang to mind. No more questions came.

The Leader disappeared . . .

The Tenth Symbol

On the tenth day the High Priest spoke thus: "The symbol before you today is known as the Wheel of Fortune. It represents the cyclical nature of things. Everything and everyone that is alive today will die tomorrow; he who dies today will live tomorrow. He who is rich today will be poor tomorrow, and vice-versa. Everything lives, turns, rises and falls.

"Do you see the ribbons flapping on the wheel? They illustrate the enormous speed with which the Wheel of Fortune rolls through eras and eternity. Thousands of years pass by as if in a day.

"The Sphinx, which is enthroned tranquilly and enigmatically high above the Wheel of Fortune, tells us that in the higher spheres beings that are still mysterious to us now observe our fate and guide us.

The secret signs on the Wheel of Fortune, itself, reveal that there is a great deal in our lives at the moment we cannot yet understand. The significance of this will become clear as soon as we have acquired the necessary strength and maturity. Then, with complete control over what is and what was, we will be able to visit those spheres where we spend time in a period between death and rebirth, resting and working with enjoyment, or with sadness and suffering.

"However, as you are still in a state of imperfection, you will not be able to remember what you have experienced and seen.

"Look at the Sphinx. It reveals the essence of those who guide the Wheel of Fortune, and also shows the characteristics which you should demonstrate yourself. Like you, it consists of four parts. These four parts encourage us to gain knowledge, will, courage and silence, for knowledge, will, courage and silence are the eternal sparks in the essence of mankind.

"Knowledge and will, decision and advancement in silence are the characteristics which also drive the gods and which, with practice, have become second nature to them. The human head of the Sphinx represents knowledge. The leaders of the destiny of nations and individuals know their purpose. We wish to know too.

"We humans gain knowledge from two sources. First, from books and spoken instruction from those who know more than we; and secondly, from voices sounding down to us from higher spheres. They either arise in our consciousness as thoughts during meditation, or come as direct messages from our guides. The bull's body of the Sphinx also tells us to work and to do, to know and to have strength. Where the will is dominant, there is strength. Our will is the source of our strength. We must therefore not only be firmer in our will, but at the same time must be aware of falling under the influence of another person's will, for we would lose the source of our own strength and therefore the most powerful part of our personality.

"The bull's body of the Sphinx therefore signifies will and strength. Our guides not only have insight and wisdom, but they also have the will and the strength to lead humanity to the highest peaks. They follow and complete their will without hesitation and are chosen to activate and realize the highest, best and most beautiful aspects of our being.

"The lion's claws of the Sphinx signify determination, courage and perseverance. When it is necessary, the guides simply intervene. However, when we see the need for intervention and wish to take this step, courage is needed to take it.

"The eagle's wings are a symbol for rising spirits. The gods and mankind rise upwards in a spiral on the path to perfection, to constantly purer and more spiritual regions, bearing the good in mind, but remaining silent about the beauty they have observed and experienced.

"There are two other figures sitting on the wheel. On the left, there is the good god, Hermanibus—the dog's head signifies loyalty; on the right there is Typhon—the evil god, the winged serpent. Hermanibus moves upward with the Wheel, Typhon moves down. The greatest truth of all is contained in the position of the two gods, representing good and evil. Good always moves upward toward perfection; evil always leads down toward both inner and outer dissolution, to end in downfall.

"The moment at which everything becomes visible often only arrives later, after death.

"However, the revelation of what we are comes inevitably. Therefore, pilgrim, have love on the way to light. Seek and practice to do good; avoid and refrain from evil actions. With goodness you will weave golden threads through the garments you will wear. Do not be betrayed by complacency, which accompanies evil for a moment, for this will slow down your own, and all, evolution.

"Now go, and come to the inner sanctum this evening after sunset: the hour of your spiritual initiation approaches."

• • •

The young priest spent the day meditating and fasting. He prayed for the wisdom to always be able to choose the right thing, to have the strength to seek good and avoid evil. He remained on his knees for hours, praying to the supreme god, of whose being and essence he was conscious, though he was only aware of the core when he was worshipping. He was lost in meditation in the prescribed position, with his back straight and his hands on his knees. The sun set, bathing the sand of the desert in purple and gold.

When evening had fallen, the young priest left the garden. The palms reached deep into the impenetrable darkness; the water in the ponds shone dully. The world was wrapped in shadow and secrecy.

The High Priest received him in the inner sanctum. It looked as though he was standing next to a slender pillar of cloud — could this be an optical illusion? In silence the High Priest accompanied him through the higher galleries. Enormous pillars with capitals representing the sacred symbol of the lotus flower supported the beams which disappeared high up into the darkness. A couch stood in a small vaulted chamber.

"Lie down."

Without speaking, the young priest lay down on the couch. The High Priest raised his right hand, and commanded: "Sleep!"

Although the young priest did not entirely lose consciousness, he felt his senses leaving him so that he became rather dizzy in a state between waking and dreaming. He saw cloud and fine diaphanous veiled figures around him. He also saw the High Priest, and next to him, the still, dignified, and radiant figure of his Guide. He became even dizzier and heard the words of his Guide: "The Wheel of Fortune turns forever."

He saw rather than heard these words. The dizzy spells came faster and faster, and suddenly he had the feeling that something in him split in two. Part of him remained on the couch, the breathing part, and part of him floated above the body lying on the couch. This was the part that thought, and he saw, heard, and felt everywhere at the same time. It was a very unusual feeling. It made him think that he was all sight, hearing and feeling. To his surprise, he also noticed that he was not the thing lying on the couch, but something else which lodged in that shell, and he was filled with wonder that he could now see the inner essence of other people. It seemed to him that he could look straight through the High Priest and his Guide, who now floated toward him.

The High Priest spread his cloak over the apparently lifeless body on the couch of the young priest, who imagined that his Guide was taking him by the hand and ascending with him.

To his surprise the ceiling of the sanctum was no obstacle. The young priest passed through the roof like a bird swooping through the clouds. This was entirely new for him. Then he saw his Guide speaking.

"Your body remains in the sanctum under the High Priest's cloak so that no unclean spirit can take possession of it: there are many wandering spirits in search of a body. They hang onto material life and do not strive for the pastures of peace. Often these tortured beings take possession of the bodies of animals or of people who must be considered as fortresses with crumbling walls which have lost their resistance and self-control through excess or sickness."

They floated higher. The city lay far below them; the sacred river shone like a broad silver ribbon.

The young priest thought of his quiet room in the temple gardens; he noticed how something seemed to be pulling him down from below as soon as the desire for his room came into his mind. If his Guide had not stopped him, he would certainly have flown back home.

"Even more than in the visible world, you must learn to control your thoughts and your will, for thoughts are forms we bear, and will is the force propelling us forward. Look around you."

The young priest did as he was told, and became aware of an infinite group of misty figures, varying in shape and color, following him wherever he went. He felt like a comet with an endless tail.

"You see how wise your teachers were when they instructed you to watch your thoughts and feelings. See how your thoughts, which spring from your brain, follow their spiritual father.

"But who are those spirits floating above and next to us?"

"They are spirits."

"How do I know whether it is a spirit or a thought before me?"

"Speak to the apparition. If he is a spirit, he will answer you, because he is a personality. But if it is a thought, you will get no answer, for it is no spirit and has only the life of a plant with the inclination to follow its creator. But let me ask you a question. Would you like to see your parents' house?"

"Of course."

"All right then."

The young priest directed his will at the house of his parents and with lightning speed he was standing in front of it. He wanted to go in, and without any difficulty penetrated the walls of their bedroom. He saw his parents asleep, but their bodies seemed to be empty. "They are not here," explained the Guide. "They are somewhere else, in the realm of dreams. Only their shells are lying there to rest."

"Let us go back up."

Borne by their will, the young priest and his Guide floated back up.

"You can see how the will guides us and carries us. Your teachers were wise to give us exercises to strengthen your will, for our will-less spirits wander in the Earth's atmosphere and are not able to go up to higher levels. However, we can go higher. Follow me!"

They flew on at great speed past the moon, waxing on their right. Fascinated, the young priest could distinguish the gigantic craters on the large disc illuminated by the sun.

"A 'dead' celestial body," explained the Guide, "that was expelled from the Earth where the sparkling waters of the Mediterranean Sea now lie. Do not tarry. We have far to go."

A star, glittering like an enormous emerald, quickly rose before them, surrounded by luminescent auras and ribbons of greenish mist. They flew so close by that the young priest could distinguish seas and continents, lakes and mountains.

"Why is it that I see only the stars and not their inhabitants?" asked the young priest.

"You cannot yet enter the atmosphere of another planet. That will come later. Your powers of vision are still limited, but they will soon improve."

They flew on and left the star shining like an emerald behind them. A colossal flashing blue mass, surrounded by a pink, yellow-green luminous moon lay before them. The colors were so overwhelmingly beautiful that the young priest wanted to go closer, but his Guide stopped him.

"Higher, still higher," he said. "Look!" It was as though a blindfold had dropped away from the priest's eyes, and he saw innumerable spirits rising up with him. They glittered and sparkled in myriad colors, most of them surrounded by white light, occasionally opalescent. They all flew toward the sun, which became larger and more impressive. Bathed in a sea of light, he felt surrounded by overwhelming joy and quivered with intense delight.

"To what sort of a gathering are all these splendid spirits hastening?" asked the young priest.

"They are purified, cleansed and mature spirits, joining together transported."

"In the middle of an infinite expanse an almost unbearable light shone. It seemed to irresistibly attract all the spirits.

"But where are these chosen spirits heading for?"

"For a high intelligence which governs the path of the sun and the planets and guards their development."

"So it is not the throne of the Almighty?"

"No. We are still a long way from Him."

"Shall we . . ."

"Do not ask. Look and listen."

The shining spirits moved toward the light in endless lines. The glow which radiated from them coalesced with their rhythmical singing to form a perfect and delightful harmony. The young priest could not contain himself. He was swept along by the ecstasy of the others, and outside himself, he praised God, for it was wonderful to be his servant. Then his Guide spoke.

"This is where the neophyte praises God, and no man can wish to harm or hurt anyone else."

The young priest wished to go closer to the light, but his guide stopped him. "You would not be able to withstand it," his Guide said.

Then they flew through the infinite space back to earth with lightning speed. It seemed to the young priest as though his eyes were covered. "Why is this?" he asked.

"Because you must not see too many terrible and sad things today. You'll see those things soon enough."

The young priest came to; it seemed to him as though he had entered his body, which was lying peacefully under the High Priest's cloak, with a jolt. He woke up.

He had not been dreaming. He was sure of that. He had experienced something great and wonderful, something he would never be able to forget.

The Eleventh Symbol

On the eleventh day the Hierophant spoke thus: "Today you are standing before the last symbol on the left. It is called Courage, magical strength."

"When you have developed to this point, certain strengths which were formerly unknown to you, and which have a magical quality, have evolved in you. You will soon learn to recognize, control, and use these sources of strength. As you see in this image, you will meet terrifying creatures in other spheres. However, you will be able to harness them because the goodness, spiritual purity, and light radiating from you will be stronger than the influence of their dark, repellent and low-down impulses and they will be conquered by the power of your personality, which may even be unknown to you. They will humbly prostrate themselves before you and lick your hand. Your enemies cannot harm you until the hour comes — and possibly the time will come when you will sacrifice yourself for love of your enemies in order to help them. Then you will be delivered to them when higher powers have deliberated on this, and evil will help to achieve the Great Plan, although it will do so in blind ignorance.

"The eleventh symbol is the fourth symbol of the path of Isis. When you have acquired knowledge from the scrolls (Symbol II) and are considered mature enough to receive spoken instruction (Symbol V), you will have acquired truth (Symbol VIII) and developed magical strength (Symbol XI) in yourself.

"You know that the visible world is merely a transient illusion, but that the invisible will remain eternal. This insight gives you courage, and by means of certain exercises, you have acquired magical strength (Symbol XI). Neither the flames of the eternal fire nor hatred and evil will be able to harm you.

"The garland of flowers draped around the young girl — the human soul — is your protection, what you need for the source of your strength. This garland characterizes the union of purity, which comprises all those who are righteous and selfless. The garland of flowers consists of only a few roses, and their strength lies in the relation between them and their unity of purpose. The emanation of a lonely figure striving upward becomes stronger as it joins together with like-minded figures. The person who is emanating this strength not only becomes inviolable, but is also provided with an impenetrable shield which will repel all the arrows of the forces of hatred. Evil will humbly submit to this strength because of the influence of one's character.

"As you can see, the lion is licking the hand of the young girl. Thus the benevolent and spiritually pure will be able to walk through a hostile crowd and no one will raise their hands against them. All others will be under an incomprehensible spell — the strength of the higher emanations.

"However, Symbol XI will show you something else, my son. The young woman with the garland of flowers whose hand is licked by the lion is wearing a hat: its brim forms the figure eight on its side — the sign of balance. Symbol I (the Magician) also has this sort of brim on its hat. With the same tranquility with which the Deity created the world and imbued everything with life (at this point the High Priest pointed to Symbol I) and with which he governs (Symbol IV) and completes (Symbol VII), anyone who has achieved a certain measure of divine equality controls and deals with his environment. Such a person disarms his enemies by the peace and goodness of his temperament.

"He has studied the texts (Symbol II), sat at the feet of a teacher (Symbol V), recognized truth, and has been assessed and not found to be too light (Symbol VIII). He has developed courage and certain powers (Symbol XI) and is prepared to be initiated and enter invisible worlds from darkness to light, without tiring.

"Peace be with you."

• • •

That evening the young priest returned again to the inner sanctum. Once again he lay down under the cloak of the High Priest, and as on the previous evening, it seemed to him as if he were on a wheel that was turning at a terrifying speed. Suddenly he was flung out of his body with a jerk, and again he saw his shell lying motionless, though not lifeless, under the High Priest's cloak. As usual, his Guide was by his side. He heard him say: "Today we will go down into the depths, the abyss of Eternal Fire, where all crowns melt together to form one. You will have insight into the way the life force works."

As soon as the Guide touched the young priest's head in a certain place and in a particular way, the latter saw his surroundings in an entirely new light. Material objects such as land, houses, and mountains seemed enigmatic, as though they had been drawn from a mist, but above all he noticed a strong bluish light surrounding him.

"See the life force!" said the Guide.

Everything looked light, light washed the earth and emanated from trees, flowers, and plants. The crystals and precious stones in the lap of the earth glowed with a soft light, and in fact everything that lived was surrounded with a glow of light. The young priest observed the miracle of this new and unsuspected world wide-eyed. He soon noticed a certain rhythm in the sea of light, a pattern of waves which seemed to come from a distant focal point.

"They are life waves," he thought.

Everything touched by these waves seemed more alive: crystals shone more brightly, flowers smelled sweeter, fruit ripened more quickly and people loved more intensely. Worshipping this all-creating and all-maintaining Deity, the young priest stared out to the sea of light, and knew: this is Life.

"Yes, this is the life force," agreed his Guide, "which makes everything grow. Everything is subject to this rhythm. Strong people, brimming over with life can use their influence to help and cure the weak, to bring nervous people rest, to help plants flourish. On the other hand, weaker people can abundantly take from this infinite wealth and life force around us by breathing deeply and rhythmically. This also explains the many cures which take place in the temples.

"Wise and powerful people are comparable to shining stars, which produce the same amount of light and emanate their waves with the same rhythm. They are constantly in communication with each other because they are one of a kind and want the same things.

"Strengthened by this life-giving force we will now throw ourselves into the abyss of Eternal Fire. Come!"

It seemed to the young priest that he became smaller and fell with his Guide into the infinite pit, but he still had the impression that he was surrounded by a fragrant mist.

"The blooming garlands of flowers, the garlands of stars," he thought.

They shot through worlds full of spirits and souls. Thoughts flew by, but at such incredible speed that he could barely distinguish anything.

He looked at his Guide, who said: "You will be able to look more closely at all this another time. Today we will visit the abyss of Eternal Fire, the abyss of burning lusts . . . ."

They fell deeper and deeper. Suddenly a yellowish-red glow shimmered around them, but the fragrance did not dissipate.

"This is the place of torture and curses, of unbroken selfishness and unfulfilled lusts. You will be safe here, as there are no strings left in your soul to resonate with these things. This is why you spent so much time cleansing your spirit during the years before being allowed to undergo the Initiation. In this terrible place only the pure in spirit can descend without danger. For those in whom lusts still rage are trapped here, like iron filings on a magnet. Habits or desires which have not been completely conquered rise to the surface under the influence of the surroundings. These glowing embers can be fanned into a roaring fire by some spirits who take a lugubrious pleasure in this.

"These spirits must stay here and suffer from their own tortures until they are convinced that their lusts and desires lead to nothing, and they develop such a repulsion for them that they simply disappear.

"Just think what these creatures must suffer! Murderers, gamblers, drunkards, liars, gluttons have all misused the life force given them and desecrated everything with their depraved thoughts. The mist surrounding them is crawling with their base thoughts, which they had in life and which now wait for them and persecute them. But the terrible torment of eternal dissatisfaction and the resulting loneliness will finally make them realize the futility of human desire and prepare them to rise to other higher spheres.

"After leaving the material body, every human spirit passes through these regions. The pure in spirit pass through as if in a dream, without noticing all these repellent and terrible things. All others stay until they are aware of their folly and can finally enter the realm of peace and light; for all spirits wish to free themselves from the earthly dross that adheres to them, and often their time here is a necessary but painful cure. The hour of liberation comes to everyone in the end, for they will gain insight sooner or later."

The spirit of the young priest fell into unconsciousness. Everything swam before his eyes and he was falling . . . and woke in the inner sanctum, under the High Priest's cloak.

The Twelfth Symbol

On the twelfth day the High Priest spoke thus: "Today you are standing before the twelfth symbol, my son. It is called the Trial, the Hanging Man. Like all the previous symbols, this one also follows from the one before. As soon as magical forces have developed in a student, thanks to the gods, he is soon offered the opportunity of using, practicing and proving them. It almost goes without saying that he will meet obstacles and difficulties. For this reason you see the Symbol of Trials is right next to the Symbol of Magical Force.

"As in all the symbols we have discussed, there is again a sharp contrast between the images opposite each other. Symbol XI showed you the sweet young girl adorned with flowers, stroking the lion. Opposite her is the man hanging from a thick branch defenselessly tied up by one foot (Symbol XII). The dry leaves and fruitless branches forming the gibbet from which he hangs indicate a lack of protective foliage and refreshing fruit. Helpless and abandoned by everyone, he hangs between heaven and earth. He will be victorious if he switches off his body and keeps the Great Purpose before him in his spirit. This will also teach you that magical forces are not granted for your own greater glory, but to serve others, viz., the Great Law.

"In addition, the thought expressed in Symbol XII should be related with the third previous symbol on the path of Horus—the Pilgrim (Symbol IX)—in a particular way. There is a special relationship; what is indicated in Symbol IX is completed in Symbol XII—the fourth symbol of this path of Horus—the spiritual path which leads upward, as though on eagle's wings. The lonely pilgrim of Symbol IX, wandering through the dry and arid desert, is now in an even more hopeless situation. He was lonely even during his wanderings in the desert; hanging upside down from a branch by one leg, he is lonelier than ever. When you reached a certain level of maturity, you were allowed to take the tests in the temple, and as you acquire more insight, you will not be spared further trials. Bear them with the long-suffering patience of a wise man and you will fare well.

"Peace be with you."

• • •

When the young priest left his body that evening, his Guide told him: "Today we will again visit a place of suffering and purification."

They went down into the depths. Again they were surrounded by a cool and fragrant mist, and again they entered a region of great suffering.

"These are the regions of wrath and hatred, where snakes, dogs and fire keep watch. Prepare yourself for sacrificing your personality."

Here, too, they saw large crowds of spirits tormented by their feelings and illusory thoughts. Some seemed to be getting tired — these were approaching their liberation. Yellow tongues of flame flared up high, and dark clouds of smoke billowed through the red glow. The atmosphere was oppressive, as though thunder was imminent.

"See!" said the Guide, "how they torment and excite each other with irritation and hatred. See how they go for each other, glowing and smouldering, and then move apart in disappointment because they cannot do anything to each other as they are all equally evil. Unlike you, they never learned to control their feelings and thoughts in life, and must now learn a much more painful and long-lasting lesson."

A little further on, other spirits were discussing or quarreling, irritated, sulking, or hopelessly wallowing in smoke and fumes.

"They must become aware of their folly; they, too, receive instruction and comfort from higher regions. Do you see those rays of light shooting through the dark mist? They are spirits bringing succor."

Standing slightly apart from the others there was a group tying themselves to branches of trees with ropes, stabbing themselves with swords or daggers, or dying from the effects of poison. However, they never managed to die completely, but constantly came back to life and resumed their lugubrious preparations for suicide.

"As you see, there are suicides here as well as blasphemers. They find even greater concentrations of the evil or sorrow they wish to escape."

"What dreadful suffering," thought the young priest, horrified. "Can't we help these unhappy spirits?"

"Blessed are the merciful," said the Guide, "and he who is prepared to sacrifice himself for those who suffer."

"How can this be achieved?"

"The chain by which mortals are pulled out of their misery consists of sacrifices. From the beginning of time compassion has driven the most advanced and purified spirits to sacrifice themselves."

"How?"

"This can happen in two ways. Either the spirit that is filled with compassion and love renounces his claim to the joys of higher spheres and dives into the misery and suffering of others to comfort and help them, or the enlightened loving spirit agrees to be reborn as a human being, although this is not necessary for his own perfection, and is reborn into a family, a time, a nation and circumstances where he will suffer greatly and have to forgive a lot. He will take on the guilt and injustice of others and pay for their sins. He will fight evil with good and in this way conquer. He will be entitled to intercede for all those who break the law."

"It is a heavy but admirable task."

"Your time will come!"

The young priest felt himself return to consciousness from the mist and awoke in the temple behind the altar.

The Thirteenth Symbol

On the thirteenth day the High Priest spoke thus: "The fifth symbol of the path of Osiris is called the Reaper. Like Symbol VII, it is a transition from one sphere to another.

"Symbol VII shows us the Deity, who, after revealing himself in the previous symbols, executes his idea of creation and the resulting laws and maintains them. He does so by creating mankind and the reproductive urge and by instilling the Spirit in the Universe. The following symbols, from VII to XIII, reveal the fate of mankind, our development and trials, and finally (Symbol XIII), our downfall, i.e., disintegration and movement to another plane. Part of us returns to matter; the other eternal and indestructible part goes to worlds invisible to we mortals. Thus death is not an end, but merely a transitional stage, both a beginning and an end; the transformer, of which the tangible part turns to dust and the eternal indestructible part continues as a disembodied spirit. Observe the position of the symbol. It is next to the Hanged Man, the Trial.

"In life, a trial is often followed by death, because the trial was simply so heavy that death was the inevitable consequence. It is also possible that the pupil has passed through the trial successfully and entered a higher stage. In this life we do not always pluck the fruit of our efforts. Very often it only becomes clear in the next life.

"Symbol XII is opposite Symbol X, the Wheel of Fortune. At first sight this seems to be a contradiction. Nevertheless there is a relationship, for life leads to death, and death leads to life. See the Knight with a black flag, the color of mourning.

"Behind him the sun sets on the horizon, and towers collapse. Leaves fall from the trees, flowers fade, and people are being buried.

"Nevertheless, there is hope in all these symbols of death and mourning, and there is an indication of the change which will be brought about by the Wheel of Fortune. The sun will rise, the trees will turn green, the flowers will bloom, and even the people will live and love, work and suffer on earth after their journey through the realm of spirits.

"Thank the gods and go in peace."

● ● ●

When the guide and the young priest's spirit had silently flown up from the temple buildings that evening, they went to a house where a man was fighting death.

"Today you must learn to know the essence of death," he said.

They penetrated the walls of the dying man's chamber, meeting no resistance. The dying man was lying down, breathing painfully. The members of the family who had gathered in the room seemed mysterious, transparent figures to the young priest.

He also saw a spirit standing next to the dying man, and recognized this as a guide from the strong light emanating from him. A bright ethereal figure was rising up from the body of the dying man, similar to the material body in every respect. Although the two heads were still intertwined, this figure had already separated itself from the feet and trunk.

Pearls of sweat appeared on the forehead of the man fighting death. Then his guide stepped toward him and helped the spiritual body to separate away from the physical body completely.

The dying man breathed his last breath, and his eyes closed. The rest of the family burst into sobbing and wailing.

However, the spirit of the dead man floated through the room, holding his guide's hand. He felt light and free, released from the body which had given him such terrible pain, especially as he was dying. It was wonderful for him to be completely free and to float around the room, driven only by his own will, and he shone with happiness.

A reflection of this joy appeared on the face of the dead man. For although the real tie was broken, the body was still influenced by the spirit to which it had been connected, and with which it had even been intertwined for so long.

"Come," said the young priest's Guide, "this was a death. However, there is more to see today than this. Death is nothing to fear. It is a natural phenomenon. An apple falls from the tree when it is ripe. The following year, the tree bears new apples until it returns whence it came, from the lap of the earth. However, visible objects disappear as soon as the life which joins everything together is removed."

They floated to a city of death situated on the edge of the desert. As he was flying quite low, the young priest saw it clearly and could also see right into the graves. The decay of the corpses, the disintegration of the atoms comprising the body, the various misty figures, some seated on the graves, others wandering about above, could all be seen in great detail.

The Guide said: "The forms you can see here consist of lives which have left the material body and have then also been rejected by the spiritual body. They now remain close to the corpses from habit until they in turn disintegrate and the atoms return to the sea of light surrounding the earth and the cosmos. Do you see how these figures flap around like clouds chased by the wind?"

"And what are the figures that seem to light up from inside?"

"They are the spirits of people. They are not merely shapes without personality, as you saw just now, but spirits of people who died that were not able to rise up to higher spheres. They hold onto earthly things because they have led a mainly worldly life and the spiritual life was strange to them. These areas were closed to them, and that is why they now remain in the neighborhood of their bodies, observing the decay of their former shell in sorrow and disgust. Many of them will not be able to remove themselves from their graves for a while. Others wander around aimlessly, seeking a body to take possession of. For example, a body with a weak will or in which reason and intelligence have been clouded. In their need for a body they will not even disdain inhabiting the physical remains of animals."

"That's awful."

"You must also learn to look at awful things."

"Are those the spirits which are called up by those who raise up spirits?"

"Yes. Admittedly, more developed spirits also communicate with mortals, but they can only be summoned on the orders of higher powers. Those who call up spirits cannot penetrate the realm of light and peace, and therefore they cannot disturb evolved souls with their irrelevant questions. They are usually connected with the spirits still wandering about on earth, who are themselves, unhappy, deceitful, or malevolent and can only lead others astray."

They flew higher and into the east at a great speed. The young priest noticed that in some countries there were graves where the bodies did not decay but remained fresh, the veins full of blood.

Puzzled, he turned to his Guide: "How is that possible?"

"These are the bodies of people who did not use their spiritual gifts and for whom the realm of thought remained a closed book. Usually they only satisfied their physical needs and led a sensual life. Their attachment to their bodies is so great that even after death they can maintain a connection with their body by means of a magical knowledge they acquired during life. At night they visit their sleeping victims and suck their blood and life juices. Then they pour this into their dead corpses in a way known only to them. It is only possible to put an end to such a practice by burning the body. Then all the stolen blood flows away and decays as it should. It is only when the spirit which was a vampire is freed from the connection with the body against his will that the victims are freed from his wanton cruelty. That is all for today."

Veils of mist seemed to surround the young priest and he was overcome by dizziness. He swooned and woke up behind the altar under the High Priest's cloak.

The Fourteenth Symbol

On the fourteenth day the High Priest spoke thus: "Life is formed from death, and life is in turn followed by rebirth, just as sunset follows sunrise. For this reason Symbol XIII (Death) is followed by Symbol XIV (Rebirth). Symbol XIII—setting sun, death—Symbol XIV—incarnation, the beginning of new life. The Wheel of Fortune turns round forever.

"We should see the relationship between Symbols XIV and IX in the same spirit as the relationship between Symbols XIV—Death—and X—the Wheel of Fortune. These two are opposite one another. Symbol XIII shows us the end of a life, and Symbol X symbolizes the eternally alternating beginning and end, life and death, being born and dying.

"Similarly, Symbol IX depicts our wanderings during our lonely existence on earth, while Symbol

XIV represents the infinite series of all these lives on earth with their inherent, constantly repeated reincarnations of the human spirit after the time it spends in its place of origin.

"Its return to a life on earth in a material body is represented by pouring water — the life spirit — from one jug to another. Take a good look at the scroll.

"A young girl is pouring the contents of a jug into another without spilling a drop, thus expressing that none of the individual quality of a person is ever lost in death, eternity and rebirth.

"The infinite sea seethes at her feet, representing the goddess Isis. Therefore the symbol does not indicate the union of the spirit of mankind with the deity. That comes later. The meaning of this symbol is merely that the content is given another form. The liquid is poured from a silver jug into a golden one, in other words, a more valuable vessel. This refers to the development, the spiral evolution of mankind, for it is a double spiral which leads us to perfection.

"On the one hand, we see the human spirit striding from rebirth to rebirth, learning a new lesson in each new life, and moving into constantly more refined and highly developed bodies, which serve as increasingly perfect tools, so that each rebirth makes it possible to express an ever-richer spiritual life.

"On the other hand, however, we can also see that a greater level of expression and perfection is continually achieved with the help of the bodies which give spirits their new forms.

"The human spirit is part of the life stream. Both streams spring from the lap of the gods, meander and criss-cross without mingling together or converging, and finally return to their origin. That is the lesson we can learn from looking at the silver and gold jugs.

"Symbol XIV is the fifth symbol of the path of Isis. Just as all symbols have an inner relation with the third symbol preceding them, Symbol XIV is related to Symbol XI, that of magical power, which accompanies pilgrims on the path through life when this power is on the wane. When this power enables us to pass the tests, we are even more ready to pour the water from one jug to another and for the creation of circumstances beneficial for a new life.

"Now go in peace and rejoice in the great comfort that Symbol XIV can give you. Rejoice in the vast distances that open to you."

• • •

That evening both spirits flew into the bright starry sky. "Today we will visit the land of origin, the land of spirits," the Guide began. "You must begin to learn about the forces which determine the transformation of spirits, for they decide, assess, promise and shape their fate." Their path did not lead through dark mists or through regions of pain and torment. No, this time they flew ever higher. The young priest noticed the movement in everything he saw.

"We are in the world of thoughts, everything changes shape faster here than in the visible world."

They flew past various spirits who seemed to be going in the same direction.

"These are spirits which have freed themselves from earthly things, left their shell behind them, and have already forgotten it and are now striving to reach higher spheres."

They came to a region populated by many spirits.

"Here we will also find like-minded spirits," said the Guide. "It is the same above and below. Death does not change the spiritual life."

Children played in meadows full of flowers, lovingly cared for by kind-hearted creatures.

"They continue here what they did on earth," said the Guide. "Nothing changes, everything stays the same. They have merely exchanged their heavy garments for lighter ones made from very delicate materials. That is why everything that is done and thought here is so important."

They flew on. Wide paths lead to huge temples, and festive crowds streamed towards the ceremony in high spirits. Masters of Wisdom were teaching in large halls with mighty pillars, and at their feet sat their respectful pupils, eager to learn. Loving couples or entire families lived in quiet huts and in larger houses.

Some families had arrived here together; others had been temporarily split up by death. Joyfully expecting their reunion they were waiting for each other. They could visit each other because their will brought them together and therefore they could always exchange thoughts, and this enriched their existence. They assessed their earlier lives, and drew conclusions from their experiences and from the fate that had befallen them. They all wondered at the wisdom which ran through the whole of the fate of their life on earth. They realized how everything in their many lives was a matter of sowing and reaping, and how every event has a consequence and every act a cause; why everything is therefore joined together like links in an infinite chain.

The more mature spirits were able to give shape to the life before them which they considered best and most suitable for making amends for previous lives, for helping loved ones, or for acquiring necessary characteristics. They could also choose the mother to give form to their rebirth. On the other hand, unschooled spirits which are not sufficiently developed are advised by their guides in these sorts of questions.

The young priest and his Guide now came to an area where inexpressible peace and tranquility reigned. A number of figures were resting on the soft moss under the magnificent trees. They seemed to be asleep. A stream ran through the cool woods, murmuring ceaselessly.

The young priest gave his Guide a questioning look and the latter answered: "These are spirits who will soon bid us farewell, for they may be said to be awakening or transmigrating. They will soon go on a great journey to the visible world. They have enjoyed the happiness of the land of their origin, they have harvested what they have sown, they have gathered strength and wisdom by reflecting on their previous lives, but now they are pulled back to the material life on earth."

"What is pulling them exactly?"

"Usually they are attracted by the love which two people can feel for one another. But many also want to return to be closer to spirits which are still detained in a material body and to which they feel particularly related. Some are called back to do penance and make amends for crimes they committed in earlier lives. Still others feel called to return to earth to help, influence, educate — though they will be misunderstood and persecuted. But look at this spirit . . . . It is on the point of departure."

Restlessly, and full of desire, a spirit rose up from the soft moss where it had been resting and made its way to earth, like a sleepwalker. A guide joined it and stayed at its side.

The young priest turned to his own Guide: "Where are they going?"

"To a couple who are making love at this very moment. A spirit who is seeking a body will attach itself to the mother until she has formed the small new body that he must enter or put on, now that he wishes to start a new existence. Birth is a much more diffcult process than death. It is far more painful and uncomfortable to penetrate a material body than to free oneself from one. That is why small children so often cry without any obvious cause. The eternal spirit experiences the small, undeveloped body which it does not fit like a corset, an unbearable torment. Crying is the only way in which this incomplete creature can express itself."

The two spirits penetrated a wall and entered a bedroom. A man and woman were sleeping. Above the mother, close to her, the spirit was hovering, longing for a body, as if in a dream.

"Holy Mysteries," thought the young priest.

The Guide took the spirit of his pupil back to the inner sanctum.

The Fifteenth Symbol

On the fifteenth day the High Priest spoke thus: "The symbol we will examine closely today is called Injustice, the Lie. It depicts a half-human, half-beast monster sitting on a black cube. It has horns on its head, with an inverted pentagram between them pointing downward. It has the wings of a bat, and enormous claws like a bird instead of toes. In front of it, there are two kneeling figures — its pupils — who are chained to the cube.

"Symbol XV is opposite Symbol VIII, which represents truth and justice. Thus, there is a strong contrast. Symbol XV is the fifth symbol of the path of Horus. It states that if you wish to reach the highest point, you must drag yourself through the deepest depths. After the Choice (Symbol VI) we become lonely, misunderstood pilgrims (Symbol IX), and get into desperate situations (Symbol XII). We must fight lies, injustice, the spiritual violence that distorts truth, or preaches untruths or casts spells on humanity (Symbol XV).

"As you see, the path of Horus—the path of the spirit—is a heavy, terrifying path, though it ends in pure light. Lies and injustice are necessary to know truth and justice, and the opposite also applies. Anyone who has suffered deceit and lies in one life will have a noticeable preference for truth and justice in the next. Thus evil also serves good in the Great Plan.

"Now go, and peace be with you."

• • •

When the young priest left his body that evening and was flying through the night sky with his Guide, the Guide said: "Today you must learn to know the movements in the realm of spirits and meet the Keeper."

It seemed to the young priest as though they were speeding another way this evening. In fact, it was not a matter of direction, but what was happening was of a completely different nature. Clouds towered before them in the dark, forming a deep narrow valley. Something swept toward the young priest, filling him with fear and trembling.

The Guide said: "Everyone who enters here must meet the Keeper."

"The Keeper. Who's that?"

"He is the product of your mistakes and everything you did wrong in your previous life. He was created by you. Look, here he comes!"

The young priest looked into the valley of cloud. A figure gradually emerged from the mist, a deformed and repulsive monster, half-man and half-beast. It approached, keeping its terrible bulging eyes fixed threateningly on the young priest.

"Don't be afraid," said the Guide soothingly. "Look at him calmly. I will stay with you."

The young priest was filled with an inexpressible sense of revulsion and disgust, the like of which he had never experienced before. The terrifying monster was standing right in from of him.

The Guide spoke: "You will always see the Keeper before you from now on, for you are a Seer. You have produced him, and he will instruct you. Every time you think or do something bad or impure, he will swell up threateningly and come toward you and fill you with fear and loathing. On the other hand, every pure thought and every noble, selfless act will change him for the better so that he will gradually lose his terrifying aspect and become a shining character of supernatural beauty, finally to unite with you, his creator, into one being.

"In the past he was always near you, but you couldn't see him. However, from now on you will always see him in a material form."

The young priest shivered.

They flew upwards. The valley of clouds disappeared in the depths. The Keeper was next to the young priest, but because of his nature, he was only visible to the priest and his Guide.

They floated even higher and encountered figures surrounded by a wonderful glow, far exceeding the light emanating from themselves.

The Guide explained respectfully: "They are those who determine and govern the destiny of nations. They influence the decisions of rulers and excite or calm down the masses."

Curtains of mist swirled around him and the young priest was overcome by unconsciousness. Then he awoke in the temple.

The Sixteenth Symbol

On the sixteenth day the High Priest spoke thus: "The Symbol before you today is called Destruction. You can see a tower which has been struck by lightning, splitting into two and going up in flames. The builder, wearing a crown, is crashing down from the window of the top floor. His crown falls off his head and his arms are spread wide. Like all the other symbols, this one follows from the previous one. It is not possible to build on lies and untruth; this can only lead to destruction.

"Destruction (Symbol XVI) is actually a reflection of the fifth symbol of the path of Osiris — Death; for the division of body and soul primarily entails the destruction of the body, but also of many earthly ties and relationships. It is opposite Symbol VII, which represents the realization of the Great Plan. Realization and destruction are two strongly contrasting concepts.

"The destruction of the tower by lightning shows that everything built by humanity for our own glorification will be destroyed in time. That is the Great Law which applies to infinity. Anything that is built, whether in the name of religion or in the name of the state, will finally perish.

"It will be destroyed in eternity and the worldly or spiritual builder (or owner) of the tower will crash to the ground from the disintegrating building and lose his crown. In fact, a crown is an expression of the lack of an essential quality of great leadership. Where an enlightened spirit should govern, only shining metal reigns.

"Work, my son, not for your own sake, glory, or honor, but for the general good in the sense of the Great Law, the development of worlds — and you will build something permanent, and as you sow so will you reap.

"Go in peace!"

• • •

When the young priest floated through the night sky with his Guide that evening, the Guide said: "Tonight you will learn to know the power of the Sacred Fire. The fire of our invisible world, like everything here, is a reflection of something related in that spiritual world containing the primitive images of all things and creatures we see here. The primitive image and its reflection always have the same core and the same qualities in common. For this reason, we can determine the nature of the spiritual fire for the qualities of earthly fire; it must illuminate and give warmth as well as destroy and burn.

"The heavenly fire you saw this morning in Symbol XVI destroyed the work of humanity; tonight you will know the positive power of *spiritual* fire."

They flew higher and higher. It seemed to the young priest as though he were moving away from Earth through space; he felt as though he were entering a completely different atmosphere. Space and time fell away from him, and it was as if he were about to experience a glimpse of the eternal reality for the first time.

Colors and shapes floated, flowed, and slid around him, to disappear in the distance. Softly at first, then increasingly loudly, he heard music around him in every key. The harmony swelled up in tremendous waves of sound, and then ebbed away in a different key or a different rhythm in a transition inspired by sadness and pain. Every note had shape and color, and every sound was spirit and meaning . . . inexplicable and yet comprehensible.

"We are approaching the realm of primeval images, the Great Secret," said the Guide with great awe.

A huge mountain rose up before them. They rose higher and higher until they came to a temple situated on a plateau surrounding an inner courtyard. A path led to a large altar hewn from great rocks, and a pile of wood was stacked on this.

In the temple itself there was a golden altar where incense was burning fragrantly. Ribbons of smoke rose up into the air, filling the enormous interior. In the background a shinging chandelier burned brightly.

With a serious face the Guide pointed to the altar, and the young priest, who understood its significance, asked: "A sacrificial animal is slaughtered and burned on the altar?"

The Guide nodded. "The sacrificial animal is killed instead of those who are guilty—the law of transmigration. What does the burning of a sacrifice mean to you?"

"I think . . . that the material remains decay," answered the young priest, hesitating.

"Certainly that is true, but it is not the essential element of the great altar."

The young priest was silent. He could not think of anything else to say.

The Guide smiled benevolently and said, "The main lesson this altar teaches us is the lesson of the sacrifice, a sacrifice that is willingly made. Be prepared to sacrifice your personality, as you have been told before. That is the great secret which the altar has for us; you will find the impulse and strength for this in love."

"When should this happen?"

"Practice in your daily life, offer up your advantages and good fortune. Act selflessly and a time of sacrifice, of great decision, will come for you. Not even the greatest are spared. Then all that is not essential in you will be destroyed. That is the purifying effect of fire."

They entered the inner sanctum. The Guide said: "Look at the incense on the altar. Does it burn of its own accord?"

"No, I don't believe it does. Someone must have lit it."

"Exactly, and in the same way you must pray that the fire within you is lit."

"What fire?"

"The fire of love for your fellow human being, for the gods, and for life."

"But — who will light it?"

"No human hand."

"Who then?"

"Ask the heavenly powers. Even buried deep under the ashes and cinders, there is a sacred spark in every human heart. Pray that the eternal breath will blow on your spark so that the fire will burn."

"And then?"

"Then a fragrant incense will rise up from you to the gods. However, this fire will also enable you to defend others, intervene for the sick and for criminals, healing powers will flow from your hands . . ."

The Guide pointed to the chandelier. "Light, the third greatest effect of fire. Do you see anything?"

"Yes, a miracle!"

"What sort of miracle?"

"I see a consecrated road leading from altar to altar and finally to the chandelier. I move from insight to insight, learn how to distinguish transient from eternal things, and see how, by means of self-sacrifice, the eternal breath can ignite the flame within and how this is finally transformed into a glowing light."

"You have seen right. That is the way. Come."

The temple and mountain disappeared. The Guide and the young priest flew toward the distant earth, driven by their will. In the infinite space they saw the constellations following their orbit. Like fiery balls the planets moved round the suns to which they belonged—countless worlds which dissolved in the dark distances.

"They were all born for the word, the unpronounceable name," said the Guide respectfully. They were approaching the earth at great speed. The young priest felt that he could ask one more question: "Can those who have not been summoned also enter the realm of light?"

"Yes, in an unnatural way, and only the lower levels."

"What does that mean—in an unnatural way?"

"There are certain juices from plants which can be used to bring about a passing division of the parts comprising the human being, like the process that takes place in sleep, death or in an initiation. However, this is playing with fire."

"Why is that?"

"The impressions are too strong for those who are not prepared, and they will become very ill or go mad. A division of the spirit from the body brought about by unnatural means undermines the strength of the nervous system."

Then the mist shrouded them and they felt that they were falling into a bottomless pit. The young priest awoke in the inner sanctum behind the altar.

The Seventeenth Symbol

On the seventeenth day the High Priest spoke thus: "The symbol I will explain to you today, the XVIIth, is called Union, or Hope. It represents the return of the human soul to the world soul and its departure from our planet.

"Again you see the young woman you saw before in Symbol XI and Symbol XIV. She is wearing the same hat with the sign of harmony or infinity (art), which symbolizes perfect balance. However, she is doing something different from her action in Symbol XIV. Instead of pouring the contents of the silver jug into the golden jug, she is now pouring the contents of both jugs into the infinite sea, while the waves are lapping at her feet. The fact that the contents of one jug are no longer poured into the other means that the chain of rebirth has reached an end. There is no further need of instruction. The pupil has learned what there was to learn on this planet, has become mature, and must now be admitted to a higher class. Freed of all earthly ties, the pupil is reunited with the gods to be trained for greater tasks at a higher level — perhaps even in another atmosphere — and then rests in the lap of the gods for a while.

"This symbol gives clear indications about the transition of the pupil from one level to the next. To the right of the young woman, a bird is flapping its wings in a tree, ready to fly away. It represents the soul, leaving the earth, never to return.

"In the top left hand corner of the symbol, you can see seven stars, one of which is particularly large. It suggests that this might be the future resting place of the spirit, and that is the reason why it is so big and important.

"Today you have seen into the far distance, my son. Now go in peace and thank the gods."

• • •

That evening the rain hammered on the roof of the temple. The young priest left his body, his Guide, as always, at his side. "We have a long journey ahead of us," he said.

The rain fell between the two spirits like hailstones through ribbons of mist. "We are in a different atmosphere," the Guide explained. They floated steeply up and saw the earth gradually disappearing from sight like a distant star. They passed countless suns surrounded by planets, majestically moving in their orbit. The celestial bodies shone in an overwhelming and splendid multiplicity of colors.

"They were all created from the will and the wisdom of the deity which have become transformed into power. This power results in movement, and in turn in heat and fire. Initially invisible to us, the solar systems rotate in a spiritual atmosphere and then coalesce to form matter. The star-gazers and wise men are constantly discovering new stars which become increasingly dense over the course of millions of years and then slowly break up, and in a process of spiritualization, curve up toward a higher plane. It is the same path taken by our spirit, but in a greater context."

The young priest would have liked to visit one of these beautiful stars or ask his guide more about their inhabitants, but he found he was unable to formulate his questions.

"It's still too early," said his Guide, who had noticed the question within him. "All in good time."

The young priest understood he was not yet sufficiently mature for this; that he would not yet be able to take in all these grandiose impressions.

The speed at which they rose was increased by the will of the Guide, and it seemed to the young priest as though they were shooting through space. Constellations and planets rose up, burst into light, collapsed into points, and became pale and disappeared.

Suddenly the Guide slowed down: "Look around you!"

It seemed to the young priest as though his inner vision had expanded. He saw even further and knew that it was all new.

If he had previously seen the individual life of the very smallest creatures, of water animals fighting, loving, and eating each other, and reproducing themselves, he could now see personal life on a grand scale. He felt related to the solar systems and the stars looked like immeasurable living organisms moving in their orbit, conscious of their strength and will.

It was as though they had silently agreed not to collide with one another. He was able to recognize the ebb and flow of the celestial bodies like a pulse. He saw fire-spewing mountains cover everything surrounding them with lava and ashes, and understood that these eruptions were the end processes of the giant celestial bodies.

He saw the influence of the planets, their emanations; the sound produced by them had an unearthly quality and their colors also had a spiritual character. The nature of the celestial bodies was revealed in the composition of their sound and light waves; some planets sounded harmonious and produced pleasing, restful chords; others brought dissatisfaction or sorrow because they produced dissonance.

The Guide spoke: "The fate of humanity depends on planetary harmony and disharmony. Therefore we can say that the existence of the people of earth is written in the stars. It is the stars which give birth to joy and sorrow, contentment and suffering. At every moment a child is born to the sound of a particular chord, under the influence of one special celestial harmony. This person will be attuned, as it were, to that chord. As the stars follow their orbit, he will constantly find himself under different influences. When they harmonize with his basic chord, he will feel well and everything he undertakes will succeed, but under unharmonious influences which are in shrill contrast with his basic chord, he will feel downcast and unrest, and ill luck and misery will be his lot.

At such times he will never be successful, and unless he is convinced of the good intentions of the Gods and recognizes their laws, he will quickly feel hopeless. That is why the wise men and astrologers are right when they say the universe is a book which describes the life of humanity which can be read by anyone. However, that's enough for today."

The Guide took hold of the young priest. Immediately they shot into the bottomless depths. The young priest lost consciousness. With a jolt, he woke up back in his body, behind the altar in the temple.

The Eighteenth Symbol

On the eighteenth day the High Priest spoke thus: "The symbol before you today is called Chaos, or Passion. It is the XVIIIth Symbol I will tell you about. In the light of the crescent moon you see a mountain with towers on top of it which can be reached by a winding path, leading past a mudpool out of which a lobster is crawling. A dog and a wolf are howling at the moon. There is a remarkable relationship between this symbol and the others. It is the reflection of Symbol XV, the Lie and Untruth. This can also be seen in the existence of nations. Only chaos and anarchy can follow from lies and deceit. Woe to those who unleash the passions of the crowd through untruthful promises. They will lead thousands to despair and will finally follow those they led.

"Symbol XVIII is opposite Symbol V—Reason and Authority. The conflicting meanings given by the creator of the *Book of Thoth* are also apparent in the order of the Symbols. Passion on the one hand—reason on the other. Chaos and Authority. The more developed nations and individuals are, the less inclined they will be to be led by their feelings and passions, and the more likely they are to act with reasonable insight.

"Passion leads nations into chaos and misery. In Symbol V, the High Priest speaks wise words to the novices who are eager to learn. In Symbol XVIII, creatures who are without reason, driven by an aimless feeling, are howling at the moon, the "dead" celestial body which does not radiate any light of its own. The lobster retreating into the marsh represents the fact that this does not lead to development, but actually impedes it or even leads to aggression.

"Symbol XVIII is the sixth symbol of the path of Horus—the path of the spirit—which gives people a choice (Symbol VI), and if they make the correct choice, they become pilgrims (Symbol IX), go through various trials (Symbol XII), fight against lies (Symbol XV), are led through the chaos of the passions (Symbol XVIII), before being united with the Ultimate Spirit—the Rhythm of Life (Symbol XXI).

"Beware of your feelings, my son. Always govern them and never let yourself be their slave. Feelings are good servants but bad masters. Go in peace."

• • •

That evening when the young priest had left his body, his Guide spoke to him: "Today you will gain insight into the Realm of Dreams. Look at your own sleeping body. The thinking, guiding, leading master — your spirit — has left your body, and as you see, your brain has the usual thoughts and ideas, but these images are illogical and the thoughts lack cohesion because the guiding reason is absent. The brain continues with the concepts and ideas which it has always used, and the result of the lack of logic is chaos and feelings which lack clarity.

"In this way we lead a double life in our sleep. The spirit experiences reality while the brain is full of nonsense. For this reason those who say that dreams are deceitful are as correct as those who say that they contain revelations.

"You know there are veils between the visible and the invisible worlds. Every time we cross from one to the other, either when falling asleep or when waking up, these veils spread across our thoughts and we forget what happened. When we fall asleep, we forget the cares and sorrows of daily life, and when we wake up, we usually forget what we have dreamed. Both that which our spirit experiences in the invisible world and the greatest madness produced by our brain disappear from our memory.

"It is only with assiduous practice, aimed at controlling our thoughts, that we can achieve a state in which we take no notice of the senseless dreams in our brain, but remember what our spirit experienced in the world of spiritual reality.

"Because we have trained our memory by means of exercises, we can, of course, remember some of the nightly events from the invisible world. However, this only occurs when the event concerned is so pervasive, making such an impression on our memory, that all the veils between the worlds cannot remove it.

"Now follow me — we have a very long journey before us."

With the speed of thought, which exceeds even the speed of light or lightning, the two spirits shot through infinite space. Solar system after solar system disappeared behind them in the dark, barely glimpsed.

Suddenly an enormous wall of rock rose up before them from this infinity of space, consisting of innumerable small cells, like a gigantic honeycomb.

"Everyone, every spirit," spoke the Guide, "has its own cell, which contains and stores everything felt, said and done. As you know, every person also has his own chord and his cell is attuned to this. The chord is the key to this cell, as it were. Everything a person does, says, or suffers resounds in the notes of his chord, and his cell in turn reacts to this chord and records everything perfectly.

"Here are the *Books of Life*. When you are ready, you can see what you were in previous lives, and you can also obtain information about a spirit in which you are particularly interested. You can also browse here in the *Books of Life*, and, taking certain rules into consideration, draw far-reaching conclusions about the future of your spirit. Now let us return to the inner sanctum."

A drop through endless spheres, then dizziness and loss of consciousness followed. The young priest awoke in his body under the High Priest's cloak.

The Nineteenth Symbol

On the nineteenth day the High Priest spoke thus: "The symbol before you today is called the Sun of Osiris. It represents the fullness of life. It is the end of the path of Osiris, in other words, of the line of thought which starts at the first symbol and continues after every third symbol.

"There are three such paths running through the *Book of Thoth*: the path of Osiris which starts at the first symbol, as we saw before; the path of Isis, which begins with the second symbol; and the path of Horus, the path of the spirit, which starts with the third symbol. Every path continues, leaving out two symbols after each symbol on the way.

"We are now able to read the path of Osiris as follows: the Absolute Activum (Symbol I) creates Laws (Symbol IV) for realizing the Great Plan (Symbol VII).

He keeps creation in eternal moving equilibrium with the turning of the Wheel of Fortune (Symbol X), through Death (Symbol XIII), Destruction (Symbol XVI), to resurrection in the Fullness of Life (Symbol XIX). However, it should be noted that on the path of Osiris not only the individual symbols relate to each other, insofar as they all constantly relate back to the first, but there is also a hidden mathematical relationship in the numbers of the symbols. All the symbols of the path of Osiris refer back to the first symbol in their numerical value.

"It is time to initiate you into part of our secret mathematics. Every number has a hidden value as well as its usual value, and this hidden value reveals its deeper significance. To discover this value, we use a special method of addition and subtraction.

"This method consists of adding together all the separate figures of a number; the sum produces the hidden value of that number. For example, the value of 12 = 3, because 1 + 2 = 3. All the figures comprising a number are added together: the sum reflects the deeper, hidden value.

"For example, the hidden value of 12 is 3 because 1 + 2 + 3 + 4 + 5 + 6 + 7 + 8 + 9 + 10 + 11 + 12 = 78; and 78 = 7 + 8 = 15, but 15 = 1 + 5 = 6, while 6 when added is 1 + 2 + 3 + 4 + 5 + 6 = 21, and 21 = 2 + 1 = 3. Thus we see that both methods of hidden mathematics produce the same results. We will now apply this method to the numerical value of our symbols.

"Listen. The fourth symbol refers to the first, and is closely related to it because 1 + 2 + 3 + 4 = 10. However, when the figures of 10 are added, 1 + 0 =

1. Thus Symbol IV leads to Symbol I. The Law (Symbol IV) originates in the Will (Symbol I).

"Now let us take Symbol VII and do the same test. $1 + 2 + 3 + 4 + 5 + 6 + 7 = 28$. However, 28 is $2 + 8 = 10$. 10 is $1 + 0$. Thus we see that the third symbol of the path of Osiris — Realization — also refers back to the first symbol. This means: The Realization of the Great Plan of Evolution (Symbol VII) is caused by the Will (Symbol I).

"We now take the fourth symbol of the path of Osiris, Symbol X. $1 + 2 + 3 + 4 + 5 + 6 + 7 + 8 + 9 + 10 = 55$. However, 55 is $5 + 5 = 10$. And 10 is $1 + 0 = 1$. Symbol X, the Wheel of Fortune, also refers back to the first symbol. This means that the changes in life, of people and nations, the revolutions of values, originate in the Will — in the Absolute Activum.

"We now take Symbol XIII, the fifth symbol of the path of Osiris — Death. $1 + 2 + 3 + 4 + 5 + 6 + 7 + 8 + 9 + 10 + 11 + 12 + 13 = 91$; however, 91 is $9 + 1 = 10$, and 10 is $1 + 0 = 1$. Thus the Destruction of what was created by mankind (Symbol XVI) can also be reduced back to the Will.

"Now the seventh and last symbol of the path of Osiris, which represents evolution, Symbol XIX: $1 + 2 + 3 + 4 + 5 + 6 + 7 + 8 + 9 + 10 + 11 + 12 + 13 + 14 + 15 + 16 + 17 + 18 + 19 = 190$. However, 190 is $1 + 9 + 0 = 10$. 10 is $1 + 0 = 1$. Thus life also originates in the Will, in the Absolute Activum. It *is* life.

"Let us now take a closer look at the symbol. You see a blossoming plain with the sun shining brightly. A knight riding a white horse is doing a high and powerful jump. He is the same one already described in detail for the previous symbols as the Creator and

Lawgiver—triumphant and achieving, ruling over life and death—as the one who destroyed the tower with lightning. Now he is leading the Fullness of Life with a flag of love in his hand.

"Symbol IV—the Law—is opposite Symbol XIX. In this case, there is a subtle distinction with the opposite symbol. In Symbol IV, the Pharoah has a scepter in his hand. Symbol XIX shows the Giver of Life—the Sun, the lord of life on earth. His countless rays are innumerable scepters which create life and laws where they are needed.

"Now go in peace, the hour of your Enlightenment has struck."

• • •

When the young priest had fallen asleep on the orders of the High Priest that evening, and left the shell of his body, he noticed that the spiritual body of the High Priest accompanied him as well as his Guide.

"Today we will enter the divine spheres," said the Guide. "The Sun of Osiris will rise for you." The young priest was overcome with dizziness. He lost consciousness to come to at a different level on a higher plane. Light shone around him everywhere.

"The Gate of Heaven is open," said the High Priest.

"Nothing impure can enter here," thought the young priest. Peace reigned, and an unbroken chord made up of three notes sounded continually.

It was so different from the visible world, and also so different from all the other higher spheres he had already visited. Many spirits floated around him. The most opalescent ones shone from a long way off. There were no dark or somber colors; everything glowed in wonder, emanating peace and harmony.

Suddenly there was movement among the spirits and they all floated toward a central point. The young priest and his Guide followed this stream. The light became ever stronger, brighter, almost destroying him.

He stayed behind. "I can't bear it. The light's too strong for me."

"Later, when you are more mature and developed, you'll be able to tolerate it," said his Guide.

"Wait for us here," said the High Priest, "and watch where we go."

The young priest saw his Guide disappearing into the cloud of spirits with the High Priest, and they floated onward, toward the light, the central point. He tried to look into this glowing core. After a few moments he thought that he could see the outline of a figure in the blinding light, while at the same time he was filled with a sense of great joy and happiness, the like of which he had never felt before. He was overcome with love and tenderness and could only fall to his knees, his face on the ground, in worship and adoration. When he got up his Guide and the High Priest were standing next to him again, their faces shining with exaltation.

Silently they let what they had seen sink into their hearts and then returned to Earth. They saw the sacred river running through the sleeping landscape, the holy city far below them.

Again the young priest felt overcome by dizziness and unconsciousness. He awoke in the inner sanctum under the High Priest's cloak. His face shone with a glowing light.

"He has seen the Sun of Osiris," a priest said quietly the following day, as he walked past . . .

The Twentieth Symbol

On the twentieth day the High Priest spoke thus: "Today you see before you the symbol of immortality. You see a messenger of the gods standing on a cloud and blowing a bugle. Men and women are rising from their graves, their arms outstretched. They represent mankind leaving the grave—Death—behind them forever. Joyfully, they greet the bugle sounds announcing a new era, an era of immortality. Death, sickness, war and injustice will disappear forever. Symbol XX develops from Symbol XIX, or, immortality evolves from the fullness of life, just as radiant health precludes disease.

"Today, my son, you stand at the end of the path of Isis and you can survey your entire development. When you had studied the holy scriptures and gained permission to pass through the gates of the invisible world so that they opened before you (Symbol II), you received spoken instruction and the promise was fulfilled (Symbol V). Then you were assessed by impartial judges and you experienced truth (Symbol VII). In this way you acquired courage and magical powers (Symbol XI), and you were able to overcome the attacks of evil (Symbol XIV). You fought against earthly laws and thus freed yourself from narrow, earthly morality. You devoted yourself to the gods, went to the primitive goddess and united with her (Symbol XVII), thus achieving immortality (Symbol XX). You have received what was promised in the beginning. The doors of the invisible world have opened before you and you were able to see behind the curtain.

"The numerical values of the symbols of the path of Isis, which begins with Symbol II, express the same reciprocal relation as those on the path of Osiris, though with the difference that the numbers of the path of Isis do not refer to the second, but to the third symbol. This shows that it is the spirit which will enlighten us, but that theoretical wisdom alone will not take us further, but should go hand in hand with insight and understanding.

"This view is also confirmed mathematically. The hidden numerical value of the first symbol of the path of Isis is a 3, for $1 + 2 = 3$. However, three is the spirit. But 3 is equal to $1 + 2 + 3 = 6$. Symbol VI — Love — is $1 + 2 + 3 + 4 + 5 + 6 = 21$. Symbol XXI signifies the Rhythm of Life. However, 21 is $2 + 1 = 3$. Thus we can see that the hidden value of 2 is actually 3.

"Now let us study in more detail the second symbol of the path of Isis, the fifth in the series. $1 + 2$

+ 3 + 4 + 5 = 15. However, 1 + 5 = 6. The hidden value of 6 is 1 + 2 + 3 + 4 + 5 + 6 = 21. 21 is equal to 2 + 1 = 3. Thus the fifth symbol refers to the third, though with a slight detour via the fifteenth, which repesents lies and untruth. This means: in the spoken instruction (Symbol V) the need for the existence of untruth is explained and accepted. In the spoken instruction we must also learn to receive the numbers with spiritual insight.

"The third symbol of the path of Isis, Symbol VIII — Truth — is an exception insofar as it does not refer directly to Symbol III — the Spirit — but to Symbol IX — the Pilgrim. Here is the calculation: 1 + 2 + 3 + 4 + 5 + 6 + 7 + 8 + 9 = 45. However, 45 is equal to 4 + 5 = 9 and 9 has the hidden value of 45. As we see, we are in a vicious circle from which there is no escape.

"The reference of Symbol VIII — Truth — to Symbol IX — the Pilgrim — therefore tells us that if we see the inescapable truth, we are all alone, pilgrims, on Earth.

"Let us now look at the fourth symbol of the path of Isis, the eleventh in the series, which represents courage and magical power. Courage and magical power are the fruit of the spirit, for Symbol XI, as we shall see, clearly refers to Symbol III. Let us begin with determining the hidden value of 11: 1 + 2 + 3 + 4 + 5 + 6 + 7 + 8 + 9 + 10 + 11 = 66. However, 6 + 6 = 12, and 12 is 1 + 2 = 3. Thus, Symbol XI refers to Symbol III.

"We will now take the fifth symbol of the path of Isis, the fourth in our gallery of symbols. It signifies rebirth and again refers to Symbol III — the

Spirit — with mathematical clarity. The calculation is 1 + 2 + 3 + 4 + 5 + 6 + 7 + 8 + 9 + 10 + 11 + 12 + 13 + 14 = 105. However, 105 equals 1 + 0 + 5 = 6. 6 is 1 + 2 + 3 + 4 + 5 + 6 = 21. 21 is 2 + 1 = 3. In other words, the numbers show that rebirth only takes place in the spirit.

"Let us now look at the sixth symbol of the path of Isis, the seventeenth in the gallery of symbols, which represents hope and unity. This image again refers to Symbol IX and tells us that the final goal of our pilgrimage is unity, becoming one, completeness, the Unio Mystica. The calculation is as follows: 1 + 2 + 3 + 4 + 5 + 6 + 7 + 8 + 9 + 10 + 11 + 12 + 13 + 14 + 15 + 16 + 17 = 153. 153 is equal to 1 + 5 + 3 = 9. Again we are in a vicious circle which has no way out. Thus Symbol XVII — Hope — refers decisively to Symbol IX — the Pilgrim. In other words, the Pilgrim will be united with the deity.

"We will now take the twentieth symbol — Immortality, the last Judgment — the seventh and last symbol of the path of Isis. This symbol again refers to Symbol III — the Spirit. The calculation is: 1 + 2 + 3 + 4 + 5 + 6 + 7 + 8 + 9 + 10 + 11 + 12 + 13 + 14 + 15 + 16 + 17 + 18 + 19 + 20 = 210. 210 is equal to 2 + 1 + 0 = 3, which means immortality, timelessness in work and in the spirit of the body.

"This is the meaning of the path of Isis. Now go in peace and return this evening."

• • •

It was night. The spirit of the young priest floated above the sleeping city with his Guide.

The Guide said: "Today you will gain insight into the celestial hierarchies. Come!"

They flew higher and higher — through seemingly infinite space. They approached the regions of primeval images which had eluded the will and wisdom of the gods when they had decided on the creation of the world and the evolution of the universe. The young priest saw a tremendous mountain rising up in front of him, consisting of seven plateaus rising in steps.

His Guide spoke: "These are the Plains of the Mighty, who know and have will and ability, who can lead and serve. On the first plateau there are spirits we call Guides and who are each given a person to accompany through their lives. There are many of these.

"On the second plateau you will see the Mighty who determine the destiny and nature of nations. Although they are further away from us, they appear mightier, as their influence is much greater than that of the spirits who accompany individual people. Just as the spirits of the first plain draw people along by invisible threads step-by-step, instruct them, and let them reap as they sow, it is the mighty spirits of the second level which unleash both friendship and alienation, hatred and war. For war (the sword) is the cause of all the revolutions in the political relations on earth. However, essentially wars always start in the invisible world, as they are reflections of the friction between the spirits of the second and third levels about the question of how mankind should develop."

The young priest asked: "If a person or a nation is disposed to friendship or enmity by higher forces, what can remain of his own responsibility?"

"The responsibility remains because within the Great Plan his own free will determines his destiny. As he decides, so will he reap the consequences. The Mighty Ones do not use their power to influence the way they sow, but to gather in the harvest, whatever it may be. The law of cause and effect is timeless.

"Now look at the spirits of the third plateau," the Guide said. "They are even mightier than the previous ones. Each of them is the protecting spirit and guide of a planet and guards over the development, the awareness, and the destiny of its inhabitants. For the destiny of the planet is closely linked to the level of development of its population.

"What does the fourth level tell us? Even greater power, an almost unbearable glow surrounds the Mighty Ones. Millions of suns rotate in infinite space within enormous numbers of planets circling around them. Every solar system in itself forms a single unit, like a family or state. They, too, are led by one of the exalted creatures of this plateau.

"On the following levels—the fifth, sixth and seventh—there are spirits of increasing power which radiate divinity and see divine things. We cannot imagine their wisdom and power or endure being near them. They have become gods. The spirits of the sixth and seventh levels always belong to the Sun of Osiris. One day you will be one of them.

"But for today it is enough."

• • •

The young priest again felt overcome by dizziness and unconsciousness, to awaken in the temple behind the altar.

The Twenty-First Symbol

On the twenty-first day the High Priest spoke thus: "Today, you stand before the twenty-first symbol, known as the Rhythm of Life.

"Symbol I showed you the beginning of creation, the start of the universe. Everything develops in space and time in accordance with the images of the *Book of Thoth* and finally returns to its origin—itself. Symbol XXI represents the end of this cycle. Everything is balanced.

"The same girl who was depicted on Symbols XI, XIV, and XVII represents the development of spirituality in the symbolism of her dance. Her hands are on her hips, forming an eternal triangle with her head. Her legs are crossed at right angles, forming a square. A triangle above a square in Symbol IV was reversed in Symbol XII to express dissonance; the triangle which appeared inside a square in Symbol VII, and is finally shown in the correct position in Symbol XXI, expresses a return to harmony.

"The youthful figure is wearing garlands of flowers and is draped with a veil. The garland is a circle surrounding the triangle above the square, finally repeating once again the inescapable truth: the Creator is always found in his creations. The four basic principles are shown in the four corners of the symbol: the head of an eagle, a lion, a bull and a human being. The head of a man shows that you belong here.

"You are also summoned to assume a high position among the spirits of power, courage and knowledge, but you must learn silence and denial.

"Symbol XXI is also the last symbol of the path of Horus, the path of the Spirit, which can now be read as follows: the Spirit, which can achieve heights where only eagles can go (Symbol III), presents mankind with a choice (Symbol VI); if we choose wisely and correctly, we become hermits, or pilgrims who turn their backs on the world and seek their way through the desert (Symbol IX). This loneliness leads to terrible trials where everything seems without hope (Symbol XII). Pilgrims have to fight lies and deceit (Symbol XV) and must learn to conquer chaos and passion (Symbol XVIII) before they can flow with the Rhythm of Life harmoniously in rest and peace (Symbol XXI).

"However, arithmetically the symbols of the path of Horus fit together very well. The path of Horus is the path of the Spirit, the path from which the passions are banned. The first symbol on this path, the third in the entire series, shows the eagle, the king of the skies, flying upwards. The hidden value of 3 is 6 (1 + 2 + 3 = 6). The Spirit (Symbol III) points to Love (Symbol

VI), but the hidden value of 6 is 21, as we saw before. Symbol XXI is the Rhythm of Life and the hidden value of 21 is 3. This gives us a beautiful cycle which teaches us that the Spirit is Love. Love indicates the Rhythm of Life, which in turn originates in the spirit.

"Now let us examine the figures of the second symbol of the path of Horus, the sixth in the series. We add together $1 + 2 + 3 + 4 + 5 + 6 = 21$. However, $2 + 1 = 3$. Once again we are in a vicious circle: 3 is 6 and 6 is 21, and 21 is 3, which can also be expressed as follows: The Spirit (Symbol III) is Love (Symbol VI); Love (Symbol VI) is the Rhythm of Life (Symbol XXI); and the Rhythm of Life (Symbol XXI) is the Spirit (Symbol III).

"The third symbol of the path of Horus is the ninth symbol in the series. A sum reveals $1 + 2 + 3 + 4 + 5 + 6 + 7 + 8 + 9 = 45$. However, 45 is $4 + 5 = 9$. This reveals that 9 is a unique number in that it always refers to itself. The Pilgrim (Symbol IX) creates his own goal; he thinks only of his own perfection and considers everything else to be of minor importance.

"Now let us examine the fourth symbol of the path of Horus, the Trial (Symbol XII). The addition reveals: $1 + 2 + 3 + 4 + 5 + 6 + 7 + 8 + 9 + 10 + 11 + 12 = 78$. 78 is equal to $7 + 8 = 15$, and 15 is $1 + 5 = 6$. However, 6 is also $1 + 2 + 3 + 4 + 5 + 6 = 21$, and 21 is $2 + 1 = 3$. Thus, Symbol XII refers to Symbols XV, VI, XXI and III. In other words: Trials (Symbol XII) and Lies and Deceit (Symbol XV) must be experienced to gain Love and Understanding (Symbol VI) for the Rhythm of Life (Symbol XXI), which is founded in the Spirit (Symbol III).

"Let us look at the fifth symbol of the path of Horus, the eighteenth from the entire series — Lies and

Untruth. The calculation is 1 + 2 + 3 + 4 + 5 + 6 + 7 + 8 + 9 + 10 + 11 + 12 + 13 + 14 + 15 = 120. 120 is equal to 1 + 2 + 0 = 3. This means that the Spirit (III) supports us in our fight against Lies and Deceit (Symbol XV), so we are able to act with greater understanding.

"Now we come to the sixth symbol of the path of Horus, the eighteenth of the series, Chaos and Passion. The calculation is 1 + 2 + 3 + 4 + 5 + 6 + 7 + 8 + 9 + 10 + 11 + 12 + 13 + 14 + 15 + 16 + 17 + 18 = 171. However, 171 is 1 + 7 + 1 = 9. As we saw above, 9 is a number that refers only to itself. Thus we see that Symbol XVIII refers back to Symbol IX. This means that you must go through Chaos and Passion and conquer temptation because you are a pilgrim. You will not be spared. It is a good thing that in the previous symbol (Symbol XVII – Hope and Unity) the Pilgrim was given the consolation of the promise that he would achieve his goal secure and unharmed.

"Finally we will take a look at the last symbol of the path of Horus (Symbol XXI) or the Rhythm of Life. 1 + 2 + 3 + 4 + 5 + 6 + 7 + 8 + 9 + 10 + 11 + 12 + 13 + 14 + 15 + 16 + 17 + 18 + 19 + 20 + 21 = 231. 231 is 2 + 3 + 1 = 6, but 6 in turn is 1 + 2 + 3 + 4 + 5 + 6 = 21, and 2 + 1 = 3. This leads to the conclusion: the Rhythm of Life (Symbol XXI) is founded in the Spirit (Symbol III) by Love and Understanding (Symbol VI).

"Now go, and peace be with you."

• • •

That evening the young priest fell asleep in the inner sanctum fairly easily. It almost seemed as though he had not fallen asleep. He did not lose consciousness, in fact, he almost doubted whether he had left his body because the veil of the loss of consciousness was not spread over him. However, the fact that he could see his material body lying behind the altar, and that he could penetrate the wall and vaulted ceilings of the temple without hindrance, revealed that he had actually left his body.

His Guide, who saw his thoughts, said: "You will learn to leave your body whenever you like. The connection between your spirit and your body is now strong enough for you to be able to do this without danger. However, you must take care that your body remains untouched in the dark: not only is there a chance that another spirit might take possession of it, but it is also possible that ignorant or inquisitive people might touch your body or speak to it. This could break the silver cord and that would mean your death."

"The silver cord?"

"Yes, the fine, infinitely elastic silver cord connecting the body and spirit in sleep holds together body and spirit in moments of transport such as Initiation. Upon death it breaks and dissolves. Therefore, as the priests know this danger, the body stays in the temple behind the altar in the High Priest's care during the nights of the Initiation. When you leave your body from now on, it is advisable for someone to be close by to guard over you so that nothing can happen to you."

"They floated higher and higher upward and approached the world of primeval images. An enormous mountain rose up from a virtually infinite sandy plain — or was it a structure built by mankind? It was actually as high as a mountain, but was such a regular shape that it looked more like a building or mathematical figure.

The gigantic structure was based on an exact square and from the top it looked like a pyramid. The four sides, which were all the same size, shone like polished alabaster. Each side was the shape of a triangle, ending in a single point. The young priest looked at the structure in surprise.

"What's that?" he asked.

"It's a monument of measurement and time which will reveal truth and wisdom to those capable of reading and understanding it. It will be rebuilt on earth, for there will be times when the majority of mankind cannot or will not find enlightenment, inspiration and wisdom from higher sources, but will only grub around in the earth, blind as moles, although they will believe that this is rational conduct. They will lack the inner light, and with misplaced pride, they will depend only on their senses. At that time this monument will speak and bear witness to the Wisdom of the Gods. It was built for those times, and the wise ones will examine it, and those who are intelligent will admire it.

"In our time there is an exchange between mortals and immortals. The gods can pass on their knowledge and wisdom, but they have decided to assemble and store the size and weight of the earth, the distance of the stars, the wisdom of the gods and of mankind in this memorial of the past and future of mankind.

"In time this knowledge will be passed on to those living on Earth. The day on which this memorial will be built in the world, just as it is now built on the World of Primeval images, is coming ever closer.

"Look," continued the Guide, "how many corridors and chambers there are inside, all designed with a deeper meaning. In these corridors every inch represents a solar year of the history of mankind. The entrance, which points exactly to the north, shows us in the first instance a period of decline for people on earth. In the beginning the corridor runs down, then a little further along, it divides. One corridor goes further and further into the depths, while the other goes up at the same angle. The place where the corridor divides is reminiscent of Symbol VI, where one is presented with a choice to go either up or down. A little further along, the corridor which leads upward divides into two again. One branch rises steeply; the other leads straight on.

"This horizontal corridor opens onto a large gallery made of polished granite containing rooms where the measurements of the universe are stored. On the right and left you can see the twenty-two square openings, each containing a symbol, so that there are eleven on either side. These are the symbols you know so well from your many years of study.

"At the end of the gallery there is a short, low passage which leads to a smaller room. Diagonally placed in the room there is a rock which is carved with a strange relief on one side. This relief is a measurement, a cosmic inch. It is exactly one inch high and five inches in cross section. Twenty-five inches make one cosmic meter. However, the relationship is such that 365.2422 of these universal meters exactly match the length of the sides of the memorial, as measured at the base of the structure, while the number 365.2422 is also the number of days of the solar year.

"This measurement was the basis for the creation of the universe, for the length of the Earth's axis is 500 million cosmic inches; the five long grooves on the south wall of the structure also indicate this.

"However, the monument also gives indications regarding the distance of the Earth from the Sun. The monument's height is 5813.01 cosmic inches. The ratio of the height of the monument to half the diagonal of the base is 9:10. The distance of the Sun from the Earth is exactly ten times the height of monument.

"In addition, the weight of the Earth can be deduced from the monument. If we go, or rather crawl, from the small front chamber to the large space behind, we will find an enormous granite trough, a container filled with water, containing one universal ton so that the ratio of the weight of the monument to that of our planet is 1:10 (3.5).

"Thus we can discover the size, weight and position of the earth from this memorial, as well as its distance from the celestial bodies and the future and development of mankind.

"By the time the inner light dims in the heart of mortals, these stones will speak, but their voices will not be understood by the masses. The gods determine sizes and times, the gods reign but people will have ears that do not hear and eyes that do not see. Those who suspect and understand will be persecuted and mocked."

The young priest looked at the gigantic monument in silence.

His Guide said: "You can come here as often as you like to penetrate the secrets of the Universe, because you can leave your body when you wish."

"I should like to know," began the young priest, "how people can work these enormous blocks of stone and lift them. Only giants or spirits could do so."

"No, not giants or spirits, only the power of rhythmic sound can achieve this. The priests have learned from the gods how to build cyclonic light pillars by means of the rhythmic repetition of a note, and using this they can raise the heaviest loads and move them, singing all the time and taking each other's place. You saw something of the power of rhythmic sounds the day that the two great statues answered the song of the priest.

"Come, return to your body carefully and slowly, remembering what you have seen."

A slight dizziness overcame the young priest and he felt himself gradually returning to his material body. This time he remembered what he had seen very clearly.

The Twenty-Second Symbol

When the young priest appeared before the High Priest the next day, the High Priest said: "You have received the initiation and now have the Knowledge. You have received what was promised in Symbols II and V. You have seen behind the curtain, and worlds which are invisible to mortals have been revealed to you. You have been shown what human understanding is capable of.

"The essence and motives of the gods are unfathomable, the secrets of the universe are infinite, but you are on the correct path. Proceed from insight to insight, from one good deed to the next, and your power will increase accordingly. Nothing that could be revealed has been kept from you. You have received an answer to the question: Where do we come from, where are we going, what do we live for? The symbols

0

Figure 4. The twenty-second symbol.

of the *Book of Thoth* make all this clear. There is nothing beyond these twenty-one symbols which is worth studying. It would be madness to seek further. That is why the last symbol is the number 0 and is called: the Madman. I do not really have to explain this symbol to you. You can understand it without my help. It represents the man who lacks his vocation because he does not hear or see.

"Instead of developing his skills and allowing the spirit to take possession, he unknowingly carries the talents he has been given in a sack over his shoulder. He leans on his staff—on knowledge, convictions and teachings—which neither help, support nor save him because he stumbles through the sands of the desert with difficulty toward his downfall. For this reason the crocodile is stalking him. The passions, symbolized by the dog (Symbol X and XVIII), to which he surrenders without restraint, persecute him and his impoverished nakedness is visible to everyone."

The High Priest raised his hand in a blessing and said solemnly: "Knowledge, will and courage have always been the guideline of the wise. And remember, your strength will grow through silence, and thus your power to act. Like us, the Gods were once mortal. But a time will come when mortals, like you, will become Gods. Therefore my son, go toward life with strength so that you will end where you began in the Fullness of Life.

"Now go, my child; peace be with you."